PEOPLE
IN THE NEWS

Bono

by David Schaffer

LUCENT
BOOKS ®

THOMSON
━━━━✳━━━━™
GALE

San Diego • Detroit • New York • San Francisco • Cleveland
New Haven, Conn. • Waterville, Maine • London • Munich

THOMSON
★
GALE

To Lily Jane, who puts a sweet song in my heart

© 2004 by Lucent Books. Lucent Books is an imprint of The Gale Group, Inc., a division of Thomson Learning, Inc.

Lucent Books® and Thomson Learning™ are trademarks used herein under license.

For more information, contact
Lucent Books
27500 Drake Rd.
Farmington Hills, MI 48331-3535
Or you can visit our Internet site at http://www.gale.com

LIBRARY OF CONGRESS CATALOGING-IN-PUBLICATION DATA

Schaffer, David.
  Bono / by David Schaffer.
    v. cm. — (People in the news)
Includes bibliographical references (p.) and index.
Summary: Profiles rock singer Bono, his childhood, his career with the band U2, his family life, and his involvement with political and humanitarian causes.
Contents: Music with a message—Becoming Bono Vox—The heart and soul of U2—Gaining superstardom—Sincerity and showmanship—Where no rock star has gone before.
  ISBN 1-59018-274-X (hardback : alk. paper)
  1. Bono, 1960– —Juvenile literature. 2. U2 (Musical group)—Juvenile literature.
3. Rock musicians—Ireland—Biography—Juvenile literature. [1. Bono, 1960– 2. U2 (Musical group) 3. Rock music.] I. Title. II. People in the news (San Diego, Calif.)
  ML3930.B592S33 2004
  782.42166'092—dc21

                                                                2003001641

Printed in the United States of America

Table of Contents

Foreword

Fame and celebrity are alluring. People are drawn to those who walk in fame's spotlight, whether they are known for great accomplishments or for notorious deeds. The lives of the famous pique public interest and attract attention, perhaps because their experiences seem in some ways so different from, yet in other ways so similar to, our own.

Newspapers, magazines, and television regularly capitalize on this fascination with celebrity by running profiles of famous people. For example, television programs such as *Entertainment Tonight* devote all of their programming to stories about entertainment and entertainers. Magazines such as *People* fill their pages with stories of the private lives of famous people. Even newspapers, newsmagazines, and television news frequently delve into the lives of well-known personalities. Despite the number of articles and programs, few provide more than a superficial glimpse at their subjects.

Lucent's People in the News series offers young readers a deeper look into the lives of today's newsmakers, the influences that have shaped them, and the impact they have had in their fields of endeavor and on other people's lives. The subjects of the series hail from many disciplines and walks of life. They include authors, musicians, athletes, political leaders, entertainers, entrepreneurs, and others who have made a mark on modern life and who, in many cases, will continue to do so for years to come.

These biographies are more than factual chronicles. Each book emphasizes the contributions, accomplishments, or deeds that have brought fame or notoriety to the individual and shows how that person has influenced modern life. Authors portray their subjects in a realistic, unsentimental light. For example, Bill Gates—the cofounder and chief executive officer of the software giant Microsoft—has been instrumental in making personal computers the most vital tool of the modern age. Few dispute his business savvy, his perseverance, or his technical expertise, yet critics say he is ruthless in his dealings with competitors and driven more by his desire to maintain Microsoft's dominance in the computer industry than by an interest in furthering technology.

In these books, young readers will encounter inspiring stories about real people who achieved success despite enormous obstacles. Oprah Winfrey—the most powerful, most watched, and wealthiest woman on television today—spent the first six years of her life in the care of her grandparents while her unwed mother sought work and a better life elsewhere. Her adolescence was colored by promiscuity, pregnancy at age fourteen, rape, and sexual abuse.

Each author documents and supports his or her work with an array of primary and secondary source quotations taken from diaries, letters, speeches, and interviews. All quotes are footnoted to show readers exactly how and where biographers derive their information and provide guidance for further research. The quotations enliven the text by giving readers eyewitness views of the life and accomplishments of each person covered in the People in the News series.

In addition, each book in the series includes photographs, annotated bibliographies, timelines, and comprehensive indexes. For both the casual reader and the student researcher, the People in the News series offers insight into the lives of today's newsmakers—people who shape the way we live, work, and play in the modern age.

Introduction

Music with a Message

O<small>N THE FINAL</small> night of an American concert tour in 1981, U2's lead singer Bono addressed the audience at a nightclub outside New York City. U2 had gained media attention and a small but growing and devoted following in the United States. Their popularity had been propelled partly by a much-hyped infusion of pop-rock bands from Britain, a trend widely referred to as "new wave" or as a "second British invasion" by the music industry. Bono tried to distinguish U2 from this pack of bands when he spoke to the audience that night: "We're not just another band from England come over here for a short time. We are from Ireland, and we're here because we want to be here, and we're spending a lot of time in your country."[1]

Chances are good that Bono himself did not know then just how much time he and his fellow band members would end up spending in the United States. Until then U2 had played just over thirty dates in America over the previous two years. During the next twenty years, they would play over three hundred concert dates in the United States, including many with over fifty thousand people in attendance. They would also play hundreds of shows to crowds of similar size in many other nations throughout the world, and sell over 100 million records globally. While enjoying this enormous popular success, the band would also be consistently respected for addressing serious issues in their music. Causes that U2 would take up over these twenty years, with Bono invariably acting as the most prominent spokesperson and activist, included freeing political prisoners, providing relief for victims of famine and disease in Africa, helping to end racial discrimination in South Africa, and working to get economically powerful nations to forgive the debts of struggling Third World nations.

On this last matter, Bono persuaded leaders in many nations that had loans outstanding with poorer nations to offer debt relief. His efforts brought him face-to-face with many national government and international leaders. For someone who is primarily famous as a rock musician, Bono has garnered significant respect and credibility among these leaders. One prominent government figure who expressed great admiration for Bono was John Kasich, a high-ranking member of the U.S. House of Representatives in the 1990s. Kasich compared Bono to other celebrities who advocated causes but failed to show the strong commitment that Bono did: "I don't think celebrities have a big impact over the long haul in

Although Bono and U2 have been popular as musicians for over twenty years, Bono is also greatly respected as a spokesperson and activist.

Washington, because they come in, have their pictures taken, and leave. . . . If you want to move government, you have to be in it for the long haul, and Bono was."[2]

A Special Performance

Their enormous popularity and worldwide commercial success would be enough to merit U2 performing for a Super Bowl half-time show. However, the show for Super Bowl XXXVI in New Orleans in February 2002 would take on special significance: It would be the first Super Bowl following the September 11, 2001, terrorist attacks against America. Tributes to the victims of the attacks were a big part of the Super Bowl activities, and the halftime show was also expected to somehow make note of this tragic but important event. That Bono and the other band members had long exhibited a consciousness of important world issues and concern for victims of tragedy made U2 a particularly suitable choice to fill this role. Throughout their career, U2 had also expressed messages of hope, faith, and redemption in their music, such as with their most recent album, *All That You Can't Leave Behind*. Some songs from that album had taken on new meaning and significance to Americans in the wake of the terror tragedies.

With Bono at the forefront, U2 showed that they were up for the occasion. Bono walked through the crowd assembled on the field as he made his way to join the band on the stage, patting and shaking hands with people as he began to sing "Beautiful Day," a recent hit that elicited an enthusiastic response from the crowd. Then the mood turned somber. Behind the band a giant video screen scrolled the names of the September 11 victims. The band performed "MLK," a tender tribute to slain civil rights leader Martin Luther King. Making no specific mention of King or the civil rights cause, it served equally well as a tribute to those slain in the recent terrorism. The names continued to scroll on the screen through the song "Where the Streets Have No Name," a U2 radio and concert staple for the past fifteen years. Bono then delivered an energetic and gripping performance that handily won over the crowd and earned praising reviews. What he did next ranks as one of the most significant moments in rock music history. Before the uproarious crowd, he opened his jacket to re-

Bono displays the American flag embroidered on the lining of his jacket to the audience at Super Bowl XXXVI in February 2002.

veal an American flag embroidered on the inside lining. This pose was used on the cover of *Time* magazine a few weeks later, and the Rock and Roll Hall of Fame included the jacket in a U2 feature exhibit that opened in early 2003.

Other Accolades

Being chosen to play this special Super Bowl show was not the only indication of the popularity and respect Bono had achieved during a quarter-century career. Bono won a prestigious human rights award from the Simon Wiesenthal Center, one of the world's leading human rights organizations, in November 2002. A few months later he was among the names submitted to the committee that selects winners of the Nobel Peace Prize, the world's most celebrated human rights award. That Bono and his fellow U2 members had made an indelible impression on rock music and established themselves as serious artists was indicated in the cover story accompanying Bono's *Time* photo. Writer Josh Tyrangiel pointed out that "U2 has, with a few bumps along the way, managed the nearly unprecedented feat of being musically—and politically—relevant for 22 years."[3] That was due largely to Bono's commitment to what he loved and believed in, his perseverance, and his willingness to back words with actions. Bono's passionate commitment and diligent creativity are character traits he has exhibited since he first teamed up with the other members of U2 as a teenager in the 1970s, and he has continued to demonstrate those traits ever since.

Chapter 1

Becoming Bono Vox

ALTHOUGH BONO SHOWED some signs of talent and flamboyance in his youth, it seemed unlikely that he would reach the level of fame he achieved later in life. Bono grew up in a middle-class, socially stable family, but he was adversely affected by economic, religious, and social issues during his youth. He was also beset by severe personal hardship during his adolescent years. None of these problems would necessarily deter someone with performance talent from being successful, but even musically, Bono had barely any knowledge or ability when he first joined U2. Yet Bono's personal passion for creating music helped U2 to succeed as a rock band.

Young and Spirited

Bono was born on May 10, 1960, to Bob and Iris Hewson in Dublin, Ireland. His parents named him Paul. (Paul Hewson remains his real and legal name.) The Hewsons had one other son named Norman who was seven years older than Bono. Although they lived a fairly routine life, Bob and Iris might have had some hint that their second child would turn out to be exceptional. In an interview with Bill Flanagan, author of *U2 at the End of the World*, Bob Hewson recalled an experience Iris had had before their children were born: "[Iris] went to a fortune-teller and the fortune-teller told my wife that she would have two children and one of them would have the initial P and he would be famous in whatever life he took up."[4]

In fact, there were incidents during Bono's childhood where he showed self-confidence and arrogance, personal character traits that would later prove to be instrumental to U2's success. Bob Hewson recalls his son at three years old walking through their garden and

Ireland

Bono was born
Paul Hewson on
May 10, 1960,
in Dublin.

fearlessly picking bees off flowers, talking to them as he held them
on his fingers. "I can remember to this day the horror of my wife
and myself. He could go from flower to flower picking up bees and
never get stung."[5]

However, Bono's self-assuredness was not always so endearing
or entertaining. He was often troublesome, especially to his father.
While his brother Norman was well behaved and serious, Bono
was often irritating and obnoxious. In *The Unforgettable Fire,* a bio-
graphical account of U2, author Eamon Dunphy describes a typical situation in the Hewson household during Bono's childhood:

> Norman listened to Bobby, Paul didn't or at least didn't pay
> attention. . . . Norman stayed quiet while Bobby relaxed

with his record-player in the evenings. Paul sang along, or otherwise intruded, Bobby was a stern father. He liked to be obeyed, and he would occasionally banish Paul from the room. Paul would linger, try to have the last word. One night Bobby lost his cool, picked the scamp up and physically removed him from the room. All went quiet. Ten minutes later Bobby left his armchair to investigate—and there just outside the living room door lay a banana skin, left by Paul, who lurked in the shadows of the hall waiting patiently for his dad to slide to defeat.[6]

Bono himself recalled acting brazenly and obnoxiously from early on. In an interview with *Rolling Stone* in 1987, Bono described how a very ugly incident ensued soon after his arrival at his first school, Glasnevin National, just outside Dublin: "I can remember my first day of school. I was introduced to this guy . . . who, at age four, had the ambition of being a nuclear physicist, and one of the guys bit his ear. And I took that kid's head and banged it off the iron railing. It's terrible, but that's the sort of thing I remember."[7]

Although Bono also excelled academically, graduating second in his class at Glasnevin, at home he was as caustic and confrontational as ever. His father remembered an occasion when Bono was about twelve and refused to use a plate at dinnertime:

> You wouldn't believe it, but we could not get him to admit that he should put the cake on the plate. The three of us—Norman was arguing with him too! I said, "We're not going to bed until we resolve this thing once and for all!" My wife actually went to bed crying at one o'clock in the morning. At two o'clock he finally said "Yes, I was wrong," and went to bed. Next morning he got up and he said, "I only agreed because I wanted to go to bed." . . . He lived in a different world even then.[8]

After completing primary school, Bono's behavior would worsen, and would become a problem outside the home as well.

Personal and Social Troubles

Although the Hewsons lived fairly comfortably, Bono's childhood and teen years were wrought with some harsh realities. Bob Hewson was a civil servant with the Irish government. In his position he earned a decent income and had job security. Yet the Hewsons, especially the sons, were exposed firsthand to Ireland's economic and social hardships in their daily lives. The family lived in a district called Ballymum, which was largely working class and strongly affected by high unemployment and drug and alcohol abuse. These problems were severe and widespread throughout Ireland, leading Bono to have great doubts about his own future prospects in his homeland.

Religion was also an issue that troubled Bono during his early life. His father was Catholic while his mother belonged to the Protestant Church of Ireland. At that time, there was violent conflict between militant Protestant and Catholic factions in Northern Ireland. While Dublin did not experience the kind of religious violence that ravaged Northern Ireland, the Hewsons' interfaith marriage did set them apart. Author Eamon Dunphy indicates the kind of pressure mixed-faith couples faced at the time Bono's parents decided to wed: "Bobby Hewson and Iris Rankin guessed that news of their proposed marriage would shock and distress their families and friends. They were right."[9] Bob Hewson avoided conflict over his sons' religious upbringing by allowing them to be brought up in their mother's church. However, the great majority of Ireland's people were Catholic. This was true among those who Bono had befriended in his neighborhood. They went to different schools and, on Sundays, a different church.

During the earliest years of his life, this situation caused Bono confusion and uncertainty. As he moved on from primary to secondary school, both the economic and religious divisions that surrounded him began to more seriously trouble Bono.

As he became more aware of the religious tensions that existed in his environment, Bono began to question religious organizations. He became disillusioned with them. However, he was not totally antireligious. Bono actually found the religious beliefs of one family in the neighborhood particularly appealing. Derek Rowen had been a friend of Bono's since the time he was about seven. Derek's father Robby was a passionate member of a religious group called the Plymouth Brethren. This group rejected what they saw as materialism and arrogance among religious authorities, and claimed

Bono, seen here at the age of twenty-one, was born and raised in Dublin, Ireland. Growing up, Bono was deeply affected by the economic hardships and religious tensions of life in Ireland.

that access to and understanding of God were equally available to all people through the Bible. Bono agreed with these ideas. He tried to discuss the teachings of the Plymouth Brethren with his family, but this caused another disagreement with his father and Norman. They regarded Bono, only ten years old at the time, as too immature and unfocused to be taken seriously on such important topics. Instead of discussing these issues, Bono found himself sent to his room to do his homework.

Yet Bono's biggest problems during this time period did not concern his home life, but his behavior at school. After he completed Glasnevin National at age eleven, Bono attended St. Patrick's, a religious school associated with one of the major Protestant cathedrals in Dublin. Bono regarded the people at his new school as less intellectual and sophisticated than his former schoolmates. Feeling unmotivated, he began daydreaming and losing concentration in class. He would often not complete his assignments, and even frequently cut classes to hang out in local shops and coffeehouses. However, truancy would not turn out to be Bono's worst transgression at St. Patrick's. There was a Spanish teacher who particularly disliked Bono. She often belittled him in class by being harshly critical of his work. Seeking revenge, he followed her one day into a park during lunchtime. As she sat on a bench eating, Bono hid behind nearby shrubbery and threw dog excrement at her. He was caught and disciplined, although not expelled. Nevertheless, Bono would not return to St. Patrick's the following year.

A Positive Turning Point

After Bono's first year at St. Patrick's, a new school called Mount Temple opened just a few miles from his family's home. Mount Temple

As an adolescent, Bono felt unmotivated in school, and he often daydreamed and cut class.

was groundbreaking in that it was the first nonreligious, coeducational school in the city of Dublin. It was especially well suited for a child of a religiously mixed marriage like Bono. As Dunphy put it, "In this educational oasis, Catholic and Protestant would learn side by side under the one roof. . . . At Mount Temple you would check your prejudices at the gate each morning."[10] The student body would also be from many different backgrounds. Bono and his father agreed that enrolling in Mount Temple would be beneficial for Bono.

Once he began Mount Temple, Bono started doing well in school. He did especially well in art and music classes, and regularly performed in theater productions. He pursued his interest in music beyond Mount Temple's curriculum, opening a dance club called the Web in a closed-down schoolhouse, where he acted as host and DJ. Having just become a teenager, Bono began to be known for his charismatic personality, and was one of the most popular students at Mount Temple.

Bono made some good friends during his years at Mount Temple. One of them was Reggie Manuel. It was one of many friendships Bono made during his early life that would prove to be long lasting and deep. Through Bono, Reggie grew close to some of the friends Bono had gotten to know in Ballymum, such as Derek Rowen. These assorted friends formed an avant-garde performance group called the Village. With them, Bono expanded his theatrical and musical pursuits. He started doing performance art, putting on bizarre shows and improvisations around the streets of Dublin. "We were this gang of *nut cases*," Bono later recalled. "We'd get electric drills, a saw, a hose, a sweeping brush, and just go into the heart of the city, in the street, and put on a performance. Just make it up on the spot. . . . We were very extreme in our alternatives."[11]

It was the members of the Village who gave him the nickname Bono Vox, which he would later shorten to just Bono. At first, the meaning of the name was unclear to Bono, and he disliked it because he only knew it as a brand name for a hearing aid. But later he learned that *bono vox,* loosely translated from Latin, means "good voice." A *Rolling Stone* article that looked back upon the time Bono was called Bono Vox commented further upon the origin of the nickname, saying it "was just a way to fit in really, alongside Clive

Whistlingfellow and Man-of-Strength Arran and Guck Pants De-
laney and Little Biddy One-Way Street and all the rest of the Irish
kids who hung out on the streets of Ballymum." [12]

With his friends, his social and academic success at school, and
the opportunities to express himself creatively, it seemed Bono had
found a fulfilling niche for himself. But his world was about to
change in a terrible way.

Tragedy Strikes

In September 1974, when Bono was only fourteen, his mother died
of a brain hemorrhage. She collapsed and was rushed to the hospital after her own father's funeral. The death of Iris Hewson's father had also been sudden and unexpected, and this early exposure to such severe tragedy deeply troubled Bono. In a 1987 *Rolling
Stone* interview, Bono recalled the anguish he felt over his mother's
death:

> I wasn't close to my mother or father. And that's why, when
> it all went wrong—when my mother died—I felt a real *re-
> sentment,* because I actually had never got a chance . . . to
> feel that unconditional love a mother has for a child. There
> was a feeling of that house being pulled down on top of me
> . . . that house was no longer a home—it was just a house. [13]

For Bono, the loss of his mother was especially hard. Whenever
tensions between him and his father or brother erupted, his mother
usually came to his defense. With her gone, Bono felt alone among
his family. The Hewson family had been traditional in the sense
that Bob worked full time to provide income while Iris stayed home
to care for the children and household. Iris's death, therefore, left
the family without someone to handle household responsibilities
and to provide emotional support.

Bono's father tried to make things work. He organized a schedule of household assignments to be shared among himself and his
two sons. However, while Norman and Bob adhered to the plan,
Bono frequently forgot or simply did not bother to do his share of
the work. Instead of doing laundry, Bono would sleep in an un-
made bed for weeks at a time. Although his father would give him
money to buy dinner for all of them, Bono would instead spend the

His Mother's Inspiration

The untimely loss of his mother was definitely the most emotional experience of Bono's youth. Her death would impact upon and shape him in significant ways. His sense of loss and disillusionment were reflected in Bono's early songs, especially "I Will Follow," the first U2 song to get significant exposure in America.

Bono described the lyrics to "I Will Follow" in an October 8, 1987, *Rolling Stone* interview with David Breskin: "It's a little sketch about that unconditional love a mother has for a child. 'If you walk away, walk away I will follow.'"

U2 biographer Eamon Dunphy comments on how the lyrics from "I Will Follow" were influenced by Bono's relationship with his mother, in his book *The Unforgettable Fire:*

> The lyric[s] of this inspiring rock 'n' roll song can be taken . . . as an expression of regret for time wasted when Iris Hewson was alive. *She* had followed him by giving her love unconditionally, his preoccupation with life outside the home notwithstanding.

> *A boy tries hard to be a man,*
> *His mother takes him by the hand.*
> *If he stops to think*
> *He starts to cry. Oh why?*

money shopping or going out with his friends. He subsisted largely on potato flakes, canned beans, and breakfast cereal. Even worse, the members of the Village would often gather and lounge about at the Hewson house during the day. Both Bob and Norman were working full time at this point, and it was common for them to come home either to a house full of dirty dishes and air stale with smoke, or to Bono's youthful and rancorous friends. This created some intense hostility between Bono and his brother and father, and even some incidents of violence. "I was *such* a bastard," Bono later recalled. "I used to fight a lot with my brother. In fact, I think there's still blood on the kitchen wall. I threw a knife at him once, actually. I missed." [14]

Finding Solace

There were two ways in which Bono sought to find some comfort after the loss of his mother: music and religion. After returning home from the funeral, he retreated to his bedroom and strummed a guitar. It was an old one that had been around the house for years, one on which Norman had showed Bono how to play basic chords. Until his mother's death, Bono had only played intermittently, but afterward he began to play more often, seeking whatever solace he could find in making music.

Bono also turned further toward religion as a source of comfort. He remained disillusioned with the church establishments in Ireland, but he joined his school's Christian Union and regularly attended their prayer meetings. According to Dunphy, Bono "stopped mocking Sophie Shirley, Mount Temple's religious teacher, and started listening to Christ's Gospels. In them he found logic, coherence, truth." Dunphy further claimed that, to Bono, the message conveyed by the Gospels "made sense in a way that nothing, not home, culture or Christ's established representatives on earth did." [15] Music and religion would both profoundly and permanently impact upon Bono's life.

Romantic Relationships

Following his mother's death, Bono also found some comfort in his relationships with his girlfriends. These relationships became more mature and serious as he got older. At the time Iris Hewson died, Bono was involved with a girl named Maeve O'Regan. While her companionship and understanding helped Bono through his turbulent emotional time, she eventually became interested in an older man. At that time, Bono turned his attention to Alison Stewart (known as Ali), whom he had known at Mount Temple for several years and in whom he had a long-standing interest. In *Bono: The Biography,* celebrity biographer Laura Jackson describes how Alison and Bono's relationship first developed:

> Ali . . . had knocked Bono back at his first attempt to chat her up. Undaunted, he had spent years pursuing her, relying on his quick sense of humor to weaken her defences and eventually he won her over.

> Ali, though, was determined to dictate the pace. Given Bono's footloose reputation, she had no intention of rushing headlong into a full-on relationship that might not last. [16]

Growing stronger over time, Bono's relationship with Ali turned out to be the single most important personal relationship of his life. However, there would be a few other relationships Bono would establish during this period that would prove to be immensely important to him. These would be the relationships he would form with the other band members of U2.

Bono's romance with Alison Stewart (seen here in 2002) became the most important relationship in his life. The couple married in 1982.

A Band Comes Together

In the fall of 1976, Larry Mullen Jr., a drummer with the school's marching band, posted a note at the Mount Temple School. The note sought people interested in forming a rock band. Several people responded to the posting, including David Evans, who would become known to the world as the Edge, and Adam Clayton. Although Bono had not seen Larry's notice, Larry approached him personally and asked him to come to his house for a meeting with other people interested in forming a band. According to Dunphy, Larry believed Bono would be a good front man, "someone with

Bono and Punk Rock

When U2 first started playing together in the late 1970s, punk rock—a hard-core, fast-paced, raw and bare form of rock music—was gaining followers in much of Britain and Ireland. The music was rooted in hardship and resentment felt by young working-class people who had fallen upon especially hard times. Initially Bono had been intrigued by punk rock, and he donned punk garb and adapted a punk persona for a time, appearing with spiked hair, sharp-pointed boots, and a chain fastened to both his nose and his ear. Bono also recognized that the punk rock trend gave bands like his, with next to no genuine musical ability, the chance to make it professionally.

Still, Bono came to be disillusioned with punk. In a February 19, 1981, *Rolling Stone* article written by James Henke, Bono expressed how he felt about punk as time went on:

> The idea of punk at first was . . . you're an individual, express yourself how you want, do what you want to do. But that's not the way it came out in the end. [Pioneer punk band] the Sex Pistols were a con, a box of tricks. . . . Kids were sold the imagery of violence, which turned into the reality of violence, and it's that negative side that I worry about.

Those concerns did not prevent Bono from expressing appreciation when some major punk influences in his early life died in the early 2000s. After Joey Ramone, leader of the band the Ramones, died in 2001, Bono often paid stirring tribute to him during U2's concerts. At a concert in Boston filmed for broadcast on DIRECTV, Bono said, "When we started out, the Ramones were the band. Without the Ramones it's hard to imagine that we would have felt like we felt about joining a band." When Joe Strummer, the leader of the early punk band the Clash, died in December 2002, the BBC reported that "Bono led the tributes saying: 'The Clash was the greatest rock band. They wrote the rule book for U2.'"

a bit of cheek to introduce numbers and chat up the audience. This guy looked right for the role, looked like the kind of guy who should be in a rock band." [17]

Bono was reluctant to go to Larry's house that day because he was not initially inclined to playing or singing in a rock band, even though he had pursued music courses at school and had done some basic strumming on the guitar. "At that stage, I was interested in the theater," [18] Bono recalled in a 1987 *Rolling Stone* interview.

If Bono was unsure about his suitability for being in a rock band, Larry Mullen Jr. was not. In a *Time* magazine article in 1987, Larry described what resulted from his recruitment efforts: "Bono arrived, and he meant to play the guitar, but he couldn't play very well, so he started to sing. He couldn't do that either. But he was such a charismatic character that he was in the band anyway, as soon as he arrived. I was in charge for the first five minutes, but as soon as Bono got there, I was out of a job." [19]

By the end of the meeting, a band was formed. The Edge would become the band's lead guitarist, Adam Clayton their bass player, and Larry Mullen the drummer. The Edge's brother, Dick Evans, also came to the Mullens' house that day. (Dick would play guitar with the band for about a year.) Their decision to play music together would change their lives in ways they never imagined, especially for Bono, who would become the most vital and prominent member of the band.

Chapter 2

The Heart and Soul of U2

BONO BECAME THE main songwriter as well as the singer in the band. He overcame his musical limitations with hard work and passionate commitment. Bono's public performances and his creativity were vital to the band's early success and he came to be its major creative force and most visible representative. Dunphy elaborates on why Bono emerged as the band's leader:

> He posessed the courage of the truly desperate. He wasn't afraid to fail and the importance of this asset to the band was understood and acknowledged by the others. Bono had [guts]. He was prepared to stand up front and present a target for the derision that might otherwise be aimed at them. Bono was larger than life. [20]

On the other hand, his strong religious devotion led to tensions within the band that threatened to end U2's career just as the band began to achieve success. Ultimately, with the help of a band manager who would prove to be as important to U2's success as the performers themselves, the band also overcame this obstacle. Indeed, while all the members of U2 have made contributions to the band, Bono has been the most front and center from the band's outset.

Steps to Stardom

Originally consisting of five members, Bono and the others at first called themselves Feedback, then the Hype, before settling on the name U2 in early 1978. This name was suggested to them by the singer of another band, the Radiators, who thought that the Hype sounded heavy handed and could possibly be offensive to some people in the music business. U2 was a name used for various things—spy planes, submarines, batteries—but it was the overall vagueness of the name, the fact that it meant nothing in particular, that lent it its appeal.

During their early years, the band met and rehearsed in a garden shed at the home of the Evans family. They made their first public performances at school talent contests and dances. They got very positive responses, with Bono's personality and stage presence working well to win over the audience. The band was encouraged to seek out professional gigs. They began opening for Irish rock bands in pubs and local clubs. They also sometimes performed at a small art and performance space called Project Arts Centre with another band called the Virgin Prunes, which was made up of their friends.

From left, Adam Clayton, Larry Mullen Jr., Bono, and David Evans (the Edge) formed U2 in early 1978.

While playing in these venues gained the band initial public exposure, it also involved some risks to their personal safety. Bars and clubs in economically hard-hit sections of Dublin were prone to outbreaks of violence, and the Virgin Prunes were a highly provocative and confrontational band. In *U2 at the End of the World*, Bill Flanagan explained that they "wore makeup and dresses and risked getting their heads busted by bottles every time they walked onstage."[21] The members of U2 also sometimes found themselves on the receiving end of glass and bottle throwing incidents. Bono was often tempted to retaliate against such hostility. When someone barely missed hitting the Edge with a glass, Bono said of the person who threw the glass, "It took all my energy to stop myself from driving a car through his front door that night."[22]

While these early performances may have been intimidating, they did gain U2 favorable attention in Ireland. The Irish music magazine *Hot Press* began giving the band positive coverage, such as this excerpt from an article in January 1978: "They impress as articulate, aware and hard-working individuals who are prepared to embark on their vocation. U2 talk like they intend to be professionals, a primary asset in the battle for recognition. All these qualities and their youth make U2 a band for the future and one with the attitude to grow and evolve fast."[23]

With powerful live performances, press coverage, and steady improvement in their musical abilities, the band earned professional success after winning a talent contest in the Irish city of Limerick in early 1978. In addition to a cash prize, U2 were awarded a contract to record a three-song extended play (EP) disc by CBS Records' Irish division.

However, in spite of these successes, the band also found themselves held back by inexperience and lack of knowledge of the music industry. During their first days performing publicly, Adam Clayton acted as the band's manager. By boldly approaching established musicians and important industry people, he landed the band many of their early live dates. Nevertheless, the lack of professional experience caused problems for U2. The band became painfully aware of this when they played at a major Dublin club called McGonagles. Terry O'Neil, a major figure in the Irish rock music scene, managed the club. Dunphy described how the band was humiliated during payment negotiations with O'Neil:

> After the set the four band members knocked on O'Neil's door. "We've come for our money," Adam opened. "How much do you want?" O'Neil asked. There was a pause, while Adam, Edge, Larry, and Bono scrutinized each other's faces, looking for a clue. "Do you mind if we go outside and discuss it?" Adam pleaded. When they returned a couple of minutes later they asked for £7 [seven British pounds]. "Twenty-five," O'Neil smiled. "Everybody gets £25 for opening." Embarrassed, they took the money and made an undignified exit. [24]

This experience led Bono and the other members of U2 to seek out a band manager. They sought out Paul McGuiness, although he seemed an unlikely choice. He had worked primarily in movies and TV commercials, but he had one success with a rock band called Spud, which, like U2, had formed with limited musical ability and appeared to have little potential.

A Pivotal Partnership

While U2 saw the need for a manager like McGuiness, McGuiness did not feel the same. *Rolling Stone* writer James Henke describes how their relationship transpired: "At first, McGuiness resisted U2's come-on's. They were so persistent, however, that he finally agreed to go see them—so he could tell them once and for all he wasn't interested. But the unexpected happened." [25] McGuiness recalled to Henke that he was struck by Edge's unique guitar playing, and that Bono "just looked the audience in the eye as if to say 'I dare you to look back.' . . . There was something special about him." [26] That charismatic quality that had won over U2's first audiences was equally effective on McGuiness; he became U2's manager in May of 1978 and has stayed in that job ever since.

With McGuiness's help, U2 made great progress as a band. The record they cut with their talent contest prize, entitled *U2-3,* was successful in Ireland. By 1979, U2 were established as bona fide rock stars in their native land. In a readers' poll conducted by *Hot*

Paul McGuiness became U2's manager in 1978, and he continues to manage the band today.

Press magazine at the end of that year, U2 won in five categories. In spite of their Irish success, CBS Records did not agree to distribute U2 internationally. Bono felt frustrated by their own efforts to promote themselves in the much larger and more important British market. Live performances by the band there were often in front of nearly empty venues, and British radio did not play their record. Undaunted by these disappointments, McGuiness helped the band organize a full-scale concert tour of Ireland, including a performance in a small stadium in Dublin. This marked the first time any band not signed to a record company had undertaken such a major tour on their own. The tour was successful enough to win the band a recording contract with Island Records.

The future was looking bright for Bono and the rest of U2 by early 1980. In a letter Bono wrote to his father while touring in England, he portrayed how a combination of factors—improvement in the band's performances stemming from their frequent gigs and rehearsals, greater media exposure, increasing enthusiasm and support from fans, a dedication and diligence on the part of Bono and the band members, and the professional abilities of their new manager—worked strongly in U2's favor:

> The band [members] are getting tighter and tighter. The nights at [London nightclub] Marquee are very successful. Each Monday the crowd gets bigger and bigger. . . . We did three encores last week. The single sold a thousand copies and for the first time we are getting daytime radio play on Radio One. . . .
>
> Paul McGuiness is in America at the moment planning our moves over there. We now have a rough schedule of what we're doing for the next year. . . .
>
> So as you can see, what was once a dream is now very real. But understand that underneath there is a lot of hard work ahead, and I hope a lot of fun.[27]

Albums and American Tours

U2's first full-length album was entitled *Boy*. It was released in October of 1980 in England and Ireland and six months later in the United States. The album sold well for a debut album without a big-money promotional campaign behind it. *Boy* also received good reviews from both the American and English music press. The influential English music magazine *New Music Express* described the album as "touching, precious, full of archaic flourishes."[28] The U.S. music publication *Billboard* said, "With a deep, rich production U2 makes music which is hypnotic in its swirling images and textures."[29]

The theme and subject matter of the songs were mostly reflections upon the band members' youthful experiences and coming of age. As the principal songwriter, Bono's experiences were prominently reflected in the songs. "Out of Control" is described by Bono as being about "waking up on your eighteenth birthday and realizing that . . . the two most important decisions in your life have nothing to do with you—being born and dying."[30] The first U2 single released in America and the first cut on the album, "I Will Follow," was inspired by the death of Bono's mother. Although not successful on the singles charts, the song got considerable airplay from college radio stations and more progressive professional, album-oriented rock stations that were starting to be more open to new bands.

Bono and the other band members traveled to America during this time to perform concerts. These concerts gained them recognition and admiration. When their first scheduled date was canceled, U2 was put into the difficult position of having to open their U.S tour in New York City on a weekend night. The show was scheduled to take place in a popular dance club called the Ritz, which drew large crowds every weekend, but of people who wanted to hear dance-oriented music, as opposed to U2's raw, high-energy kind of rock. That tour was handled by the Premier Talent Agency, a company headed by a well-established concert touring manager named Frank Barsalona. In his book *U2: The Road to Pop,* musical journalist Carter Alan said that Barsalona was "prepared for a possible disaster" under the circumstances. Instead, Barsalona was amazed and thrilled by what he witnessed. "With every song . . . a little part of the audience started paying attention. . . . When they were about sixty percent through they basically had the whole audience. . . . I still get chills thinking about it."[31]

U2 had a similarly amazing experience at a live performance in Boston. Booked as the opening act for an American band named Barooga, which had received greater airplay and promotion from the sponsoring Boston radio station, U2 once again enthralled the crowd. When their relatively short allotted time was up, the audience was so wild and enthusiastic that U2 were permitted to play an encore. Even then the crowd was ravenous for more, so to their astonishment, the band was escorted back out from their dressing room by the stage manager to play yet another encore. In his astonishment, Bono gaspingly said to the crowd, "This is our first ever . . . I don't know what!"[32]

Bono, seen here in 1983, has been U2's principal songwriter, drawing primarily on personal experience as subject matter.

Bono's Bombast

During these early performances, Bono's stage presence and energetic performance were the focal point and were mostly what elicited such enthusiastic responses from the crowds. The Edge commented on this in a *Rolling Stone* article:

> I think he did something that not many others did, and that was confront a crowd. Around that era, most bands were basically as good as their material. Bono was different. He went out there and he *assumed* this importance and this character and eyed the audience and was totally impressive—even though nothing behind him backed him up.[33]

U2 performs at Super Bowl XXXVI. Bono's stage presence and high energy have always been the focal point of the band's performances.

U2's stunning success in their first ever U.S. tour prompted their record company to provide substantial financial and promotional support for the band's next tour of America in the spring of 1981. This tour was far more extensive, covering every region of the country and playing to larger audiences. In between these two American tours, the band kept playing frequently in Britain and elsewhere in Europe. They also played those places again after completing the second set of live American dates.

The release of U2's second album, *October,* came appropriately in October of 1981. Once again the band embarked on a nationwide tour to promote the new album. While the live performances continued to be enthusiastically received and positively reviewed, reactions to the *October* album were more mixed. Overall though, U2 could justifiably feel proud of how far they had come in the five years they had been together.

Then again, they had also set lofty goals for themselves, goals that they had not yet reached. In an early 1981 interview, Bono had said, "I do feel we're meant to be one of the great groups. There's a certain spark, a certain chemistry, that was special about the Stones, the Who and the Beatles, and I think it's also special about U2."[34] If attaining that level of success was what Bono was after, the band would need to achieve far more than they had. They were still quite young and had time enough to attain that level of greatness, but conflicts and tensions within the band threatened to cut short that opportunity.

Conflict over Christianity

Bono's strong religious convictions had certainly played a major role in his life since he started working with U2. His spiritual side was even subtly revealed in the songs on the band's first two records. On *October* though, Bono's religious beliefs were vibrantly proclaimed. He employed Latin hymnal lyrics proclaiming God great and glorious, and celebrated the joy and liberation of giving himself over to a higher power. The song "With a Shout" was almost strident in its imagery of biblical apocalypse and exaltation of a return to Jerusalem. There was a reason behind this new overt religiousness in Bono's songwriting.

Rockin' Religion

Christian religious references in U2's music were most prevalent on their second album, *October,* but there have been a number of U2 songs since then that reveal Bono's beliefs. On the *War* album, the closing song "40" was inspired by Psalm 40 in the Bible. The song's lyrics are closely derived from this original Bible text, quoted from the Authorized (King James) Version:

> I waited patiently for the Lord; and he inclined unto me, and heard my cry.

> He brought me up also out of an horrible pit, out of the miry clay, and set my feet upon a rock, *and* established my goings.

> And he hath put a new song in my mouth, even praise unto our God: many shall see see it, and fear, and shall trust in the [Lord].

For many years "40" was the song U2 used to close all their concerts, and the crowds invariably joined in to sing along with Bono during the refrain.

Christian references appear in the No. 1 hit song from *The Joshua Tree,* "I Still Haven't Found What I'm Looking For." In the song, Bono proclaims his faith by mentioning the Crucifixion and the Second Coming of Christ. A gospel choir from New York City called the New Voices of Freedom also performed the song, and together with U2 they recorded a joint version that appears on the *Rattle and Hum* album.

After *The Joshua Tree,* Bono rarely made such overt references to Christian creeds or images in his songs. One exception was the song "Beautiful Day," which was another No. 1 hit for U2 in 2000. The lyrics include a vivid reference to the biblical flood described in the Book of Genesis.

In between the two U2 tours of America, Bono had become part of a charismatic Christian group called Shalom. Two friends of his from the Village, Gucci and Pod, had gotten involved with it, and through them Bono had become interested. He in turn recruited fellow band members Larry Mullen and the Edge, both of whom also had strong spiritual inclinations. Although Adam Clayton was also somewhat religious and was welcomed by Bono to join the Shalom group, he found no appeal in it. As the other three band members became more deeply involved in the group, a division formed in the band. Furthermore, the three devout members of U2 began to wonder if they could live a rock music lifestyle and be true to their faith.

In *The Unforgettable Fire,* Dunphy describes how this conflict came to bear heavily upon Bono: "One of the tenets of Shalom's

Christianity was the surrender of ego so that you might be filled with the Spirit of God. U2 were a big band in Ireland now, Bono in particular its public face. How could he reconcile that with his love of God? Most of those at the Meetings lived ordinary lives. Their days were dull, some particularly sad and lonely."[35]

The Edge and Larry Mullen also had to reconcile the differences between rock music culture and their spiritual beliefs. Rather than yield to the pressure to give up music, these three members of U2 resolved to try to compromise: They would continue to create and play rock music, but would eschew the decadent excesses often associated with it, such as promiscuous sex and drug use. Difficult though it may seem, Bono, the Edge, and Mullen were determined, as Dunphy put it, to "bridge the gap between the rock 'n' roll they loved and the Christian ethos they were committed to."[36]

Bono commented of this spiritual devotion in a letter to his father:

> You should be aware that at the moment three of the group are committed Christians. That means offering each day up to God, meeting in the morning for prayers, readings, and letting God work in our lives. This gives us strength and a joy that does not depend on drink or drugs. This strength will, I believe, be the quality that will take us to the top of the music business. I hope our lives will be a testament to the people who follow us, and to the music business. . . . It is our ambition to make more than good music.
>
> I know that you must find this a ludicrous ambition, but compared to the task of getting ourselves from where we were to where we are, the rest is easy.[37]

However, problems linked to the three members' new devotion emerged during a U.S. tour in early 1981. Bono, the Edge, and Mullen regularly held prayer meetings and sang religious songs together on the tour bus, away from the rest of the touring party but unavoidably within sight and earshot. This caused discomfort for many among the crew and management staff. For

Adam Clayton, it created feelings of severe isolation and insecurity. Clayton enjoyed an active social life and the high profile that came with being a rock star. As Dunphy states, "This was a way of life directly in conflict with the one now being celebrated . . . at the back of the bus."[38] Clayton went so far as to wonder whether U2 had become a Christian band, and if there was still a place in it for him.

With the recording and release of *October,* the public became aware of U2's Christianity. It became the subject of much media coverage and fan conversation. The tension between the other three members and Clayton intensified.

A Managerial Feat

This situation came to a head in November 1981, when Bono, the Edge, and Mullen went to Paul McGuiness with the shocking news that they had concluded they could not reconcile their religious beliefs with being in the business. They decided not to proceed with the worldwide tour that had been planned to support the newly released *October.* During the uneasiness of the previous months, McGuiness had been supportive of Clayton and had disliked the way he was excluded by the other band members. Yet when confronted with this announcement, McGuiness reacted rationally. He pointed out that, acting on the band's behalf, he had committed the band to playing many tour dates in both America and Europe during the coming year. He also pointed out that others had also committed themselves for the sake of the band:

> Promoters were committed, as was their own crew. . . . There were an awful lot of people committed to U2. The band had majored on its integrity. How could they possibly renege on their obligations now? Paul couldn't see how those who were encouraging Bono, Larry and Edge to walk away from these obligations could square such an act with Christianity. . . . If they wanted to quit rock 'n' roll it could be done, but it should be done properly. U2 could be phased out, the band couldn't simply drop out. To do so would be to deny everything they stood for.[39]

Despite religious differences and personality conflicts, the original members of U2 have remained together for over twenty years.

With these strong arguments, McGuiness convinced the band members not to abandon U2 right away. He sensed that they would change their minds as time went on, and was proven correct. When the band began touring in the United States again, there were no indications that any of them still wanted to give up a musical career. In fact, Bono frequently told their American audiences that the band planned on spending a lot of time in their country. It certainly appeared that U2 intended to be around for a long time to come.

Getting Married

The conflicts over Christianity and their resolution helped solid-
ify Bono's personal and professional relationships with his fellow
band members and their manager. Another very important relationship in Bono's life was solidified on August 21, 1982, when
Bono married his girlfriend from the Mount Temple School, Alison
Stewart. In what Dunphy called "a generous gesture of reconcil-
iation, a public declaration of friendship and respect,"[40] Bono had
Clayton serve as his best man. All of Bono's friends from the
Village, some of whom had had their own differences over membership in the Shalom group, also attended. Bono's father and
brother were also present, their past differences likewise forgot-
ten.

Bono and Ali's wedding proved to be a great and celebratory
gathering of all the important people in Bono's life. The personal
and working relationships Bono had established with these people would prove to be long lasting and important to him and would
also prove critical in his rise to stardom.

Chapter 3

Gaining Superstardom

$\mathbf{A}$s U2 BUILT upon their early success and progressed both artistically and professionally, Bono became an increasingly well-known personality. This fame built to the point where he was among the most famous and successful music stars in the world. For a time, his live performances became more flamboyant, even dangerous, and this was one means by which he began gaining a higher public profile. At the same time, Bono also began to establish and further his reputation as a serious, conscientious songwriter and spokesperson on important social and political issues.

Political Performance

After experiencing uncertainty about his future with the band and ultimately reconfirming his commitment, Bono took a major step forward in his career by including political messages in his songs and performances. During a show in Belfast, Northern Ireland, in December 1982, Bono paused to introduce a new song to the audience: "Listen, this is called 'Sunday Bloody Sunday.' It's not a rebel song. It's a song of hope and a song of disgust."[41] U2 had been playing the song during a month-long tour to introduce music from their forthcoming album to be released in early 1983, but the song had special significance in Northern Ireland. Although the song has been subject to many interpretations, its most obvious reference was to events that took place in Northern Ireland. The song discussed the violence between Irish Nationalists, who wanted Northern Ireland to unite with Ireland into one nation, and British military forces acting on behalf of the Protestant majority in Northern Ireland, who wanted to remain separate from Ireland and a part of the United Kingdom.

One of the world's most famous and successful music stars, Bono has used his fame to bring attention to various political and social issues.

The song's lyrics were vivid, describing combat debris flying in front of children and dead bodies strewn on the ground. The conflict in Northern Ireland centered on differences between Catholics and Protestants, and coming from a family with parents of different faiths, the song's lyrics also spoke to Bono's own sense of personal conflict growing up. Bono made it clear in both the song's lyrics and in comments he made about the song that he intended not to take either side in the conflict, but simply to express his distress and anguish over it. In the June 9, 1983, *Rolling Stone* article, Bono is quoted as saying that "The bitterness between those two communities is ridiculous. . . . I see in both . . . aspects of things I don't fully like. But I like to think that I'd be able to go to a Catholic church or a Protestant church." [42]

"Sunday Bloody Sunday" marked the emergence of political overtones in Bono's songwriting, and there would be more political references in the new album, entitled *War,* which was released in February 1983. For instance, "New Year's Day" was a song about

Bloody Sunday in Ireland

There were two days during the twentieth century known in Ireland as Bloody Sunday, but only one took place during Bono's lifetime. On January 30, 1972, in Derry, Northern Ireland, an elite British Paratroop Regiment opened fire upon a crowd demonstrating in favor of Northern Irish independence from the United Kingdom. Fourteen people were killed and many more were wounded. Bitterness and hatred raged between militant Catholic and Protestant factions for decades afterward, and a terrorist group called the Irish Republican Army undertook a prolonged bombing campaign in England.

The British forces defended the action. The commander of British forces in Northern Ireland was quoted by Bernard Weinraub in the February 1, 1972, *New York Times* article entitled "Ulster Catholics Protest Killings; Reprisals Vowed" as saying, "There is absolutely no doubt that the parachute battalion opened up only after they had been fired on. Unfortunately, a hooligan element took over and attacked our troops." A clerical Catholic leader denied this, however, saying in the same article that the British troops "shot indiscriminately and everywhere around them without any provocation."

Although he was a good distance away from these troubles down in Dublin, the conflict between Catholics and Protestants in Northern Ireland disturbed Bono, especially as the conflict persisted through his adolescence and into adulthood. In *U2: Into the Heart: The Stories Behind Every Song,* author Niall Stokes quotes Bono explaining how he expressed his exasperation and sense of futility over the violence in the song "Sunday Bloody Sunday": "What I was trying to say in the song is . . . I'm sick of it. How long must it go on? It's a statement. I'm not even saying there's an answer."

the struggle in Poland by laborers against what was then a Communist government. The song "Seconds" dealt with nuclear war and the international political intimidation made possible by nuclear weapons.

New Public Perceptions

The new album also represented progress for the band commercially. It debuted at the top of the British album charts and reached No. 12 in the United States. The song "New Year's Day" also became U2's first song to chart on the critically important *Billboard* magazine Hot 100. In addition, the news and entertainment media began taking U2 more seriously. A *Washington Post* article reviewing three recently released rock albums dealing with the issue of war was most favorable to U2. Writer Richard Harrington described the music as having "a rough hewn energy built on a solid rock bottom." On the album's sociopolitical content, Harrington commented that "Bono and his generation have come of age with 'trenches dug within our hearts,' [lyrics from "Sunday Bloody Sunday"] but his own sense of Christian hope and redemption never fails him."[43]

Bono also started being taken seriously by government officials following the *War* album. In November 1983, Irish prime minister Garret Fitzgerald asked Bono to serve on a national committee on the severe unemployment problem in Ireland. Bono accepted the position. However, he soon quit this post out of dissatisfaction with the way the committee operated. He explained his frustration in a 1985 interview: "There were good people there . . . but there was another language I had to come up with, which is committeespeak. . . . I could go off and do all these things and right wrongs and go into a committee, but that's not where I am. I'm realizing that I've got to find where I am."[44]

Excessive Onstage Exuberance

While Bono was growing musically and as a humanitarian, there was still a youthful part of him that was restless, even reckless. This aspect of Bono's personality increasingly portrayed itself during U2's live performances. During the early to mid-1980s, he took ac-

Bono's onstage exuberance has always delighted U2 fans. The singer's showmanship is a key factor in the band's continued success.

tions onstage that were risky and hazardous both to himself and to others onstage with him and to those in the audience.

Bono's high-energy stage performances had always been the most exciting part of U2's shows and critical to the band's success. His close contact with the audience won support among fans and attracted others to U2. Increasingly large and more boisterous crowds turned out for their shows, but U2 was still playing small places and working with minimum security. Concerns began to rise when Bono starting climbing on scaffolding and speakers while performing. During one particular song, "Electric Co.," Bono often waved a white flag while running and jumping around the stage and into the audience. At a show in Albany, New York, in 1983, Bono climbed to the top of the scaffolding and planted a white flag in an open fixture. A few nights later, a more frightening incident occurred at a show in New Haven, Connecticut. This incident is described in Alan's *U2: The Road to Pop:*

> Bono grabbed the white flag and ascended the left PA stacks.
> . . . [The road manager's] eyes widened in alarm as Bono abruptly leapt across the three-foot gulf onto the balcony.
> . . . Bono paraded along the foot-wide balcony between astonished fans and a thirty-foot drop to the crowd below. When he knelt on the narrow ledge and began singing fans held onto him to prevent a possible fall. Bono stood up, pivoted and returned the way he had come. . . . After Bono completed a jump back onto the speaker stack, which wobbled somewhat under the impact, [the road manager] visibly relaxed. [45]

Bono's stunts continued to cause a major stir that summer when U2 performed at the US Festival in Southern California, a four-day, outdoor concert event. U2 appeared before one hundred thousand people. During the band's set, Bono ascended on a rope ladder 120 feet above the center stage and stood above a massive US Festival banner. To the astonishment of everyone at the show, Bono sang from this perch as he planted two flags, a white one and an Irish one, above the banner. Among those shocked and amazed by this were the other members of U2. "I tell you, he made us so scared," claimed the Edge in an interview with Carter Alan following the show. "He didn't tell us he was going to do it. Maybe he didn't know he was going to do it himself. Myself, Adam, and Larry were down there, mouths open, just waiting to see what was going to happen." [46]

At this point, the entire production and management crew had come to consider Bono's outrageous stunts a grave matter. Ellen Darst, who handled much of the band's business in America, commented on this:

> There was pressure on [Bono]; he had to feel that he could play these places [arenas, stadiums, and festivals] and still

reach people. He kept feeling pushed to do these grand moves to be seen. There was ongoing disagreement about whether or not this was what should be happening. Everybody felt it was dangerous, wasn't necessary, or worth the risk. [47]

Bono himself believed he went too far after an ugly incident at a Los Angeles show. After walking onto the balcony from a platform behind the stage with a white flag and a microphone, Bono found himself cut off from his path back by fighting fans. Standing at the edge of the balcony, Bono threatened to jump down twenty feet if the fighting did not stop. The fighting persisted, so Bono jumped with the flag and microphone. This set off a frenzy in which many fans followed his lead and jumped from the balcony. Bodies piled up on top of the seats below, and Bono found himself trapped. The flag was torn away from him and his own shirt was ripped. Bono fought off those crushing him until security cleared the scene and escorted Bono safely back to the stage. Bono said afterward: "I lost my senses completely. . . . Someone could have died at that concert, and it was a real sickener for me. It's meant a total reevaluation of what we are about live." [48]

New Road and Record Successes

Though Bono's flamboyance may have caused considerable distress among those involved with the concert tour, there was no question that, with the US Festival performance in particular, his actions had also gained widespread attention and admiration for the band. Other positive results from the War tour included a live video performance and live minirecording, both entitled *Under a Blood Red Sky,* the title taken from a lyric in the song "New Year's Day." The video performance took place at Red Rocks Amphitheater in Colorado. The video was nominated for an award by *Billboard* magazine, and the album reached the Top 30 on the charts in both Britain and America.

The band's next full-length album was released the following year, in 1984. To help them expand upon their previously raw and

hard-driving sound, they employed Brian Eno, a musician and producer known for his technical wizardry, innovation, and ambient
sound style. Entitled *The Unforgettable Fire,* the album's differences
with its predecessors were distinct. Although some of the songs were
still high-energy rhythmic rockers, overall the album had a mel-
lower, smoother, more textured quality. This did not go over well

U2 hired Brian Eno to produce their album The Unforgettable Fire.
*Although distinctly different from U2's previous work, the album was
well received by fans.*

with all reviewers. *Rolling Stone's* Kurt Loder claimed the album was hampered by "a misconceived production strategy and occasional interludes of soggy, songless self-indulgence."[49] Still the album equaled the success of *War,* peaking at No. 1 on the British charts and No. 12 in the United States. The single "Pride (In the Name of Love)" from the album reached the Top 3 on the British charts and became the band's first U.S. Top 40 hit.

With Bono again providing most of the creative contribution to the album, the songs reflected continued growth on his part, both as a songwriter and a social observer. "Pride" and another song on the album, "MLK," both were tributes to slain American civil rights leader Martin Luther King Jr. The song "Bad" dealt with the damage and pain caused by drug abuse that Bono had witnessed in his own Ballymum neighborhood in Dublin. There were more songs dealing with nuclear war, including the title track. This title was taken from the name of an art exhibit shown at a place called the Peace Museum in Chicago, where U2 had visited during their time in America. The exhibit featured artwork by survivors of the nuclear attacks on Japan at the end of World War II.

In his book *U2: Into the Heart: The Stories Behind Every Song,* longtime U2 friend Niall Stokes quotes the Edge regarding how witnessing these images affected Bono. "Painting was part of the therapy to help these people purge themselves of their internalized emotions. . . . The image of that purging quality, coupled with the insight it gave into the horror of nuclear holocaust, stuck in Bono's mind."[50] In fact, Bono became a major proponent of the Peace Museum, and helped get *The Unforgettable Fire* exhibit displayed in Ireland.

Road to the Top

Returning to the road after the album's release, U2 continued to identify with social and political causes, starting off with a limited U.S. tour during which they donated all the proceeds to Amnesty International, a worldwide organization dedicated to aiding political prisoners and victims of government torture. While continuing to tour in Europe in the spring of 1985, U2 received a most notable distinction: They were named by *Rolling Stone* as the "Band of the Eighties." In the accompanying article, writer Christopher Connelly elaborated upon this prestigious designation:

> In America . . . they have yet to notch a Top Ten album or single. Only now are they beginning to tour arena-size venues. But for a growing number of rock & roll fans U2 . . . has become the band that matters most, maybe even the *only* band that matters. It's no coincidence that U2 sells more T-shirts and merchandise than groups that sell twice as many records, or that four of U2's five albums are currently on *Billboard's* Top 200. The group has become one of the handful of artists in rock & roll history . . . that people are eager to identify themselves with. And they've done it not just with their music but with a larger message as well—by singing "Pride (In the Name of Love)" while most other groups sing about pride in an act of love.[51]

Now firmly established as a successful rock band, thrilling live performers, and socially conscientious artists, U2 seemed a natural choice for a major, multi-arena concert that summer called Live Aid, which was intended to raise money to help famine victims in Ethiopia. The event took place in July 1985, with a multitude of big-name artists playing at Wembley Stadium in London and Robert F. Kennedy Stadium in Philadelphia. Spectators in both venues could watch the performances at the other venue on large video screens. The entire show was broadcast on worldwide television, with appeals for contributions made by celebrities during breaks between acts.

Their performance at Live Aid is considered another major event for U2, and it provided the largest audience yet to witness Bono's showmanship. After U2 had delivered a dramatic rendition of "Sunday Bloody Sunday," Bono, who had been restraining himself during The Unforgettable Fire tour and not engaging in the kind of antics that had caused problems previously, once again acted spontaneously. During a performance of the song "Bad," he jumped from the stage onto a lower-level pit area full of press and security people. Spotting people in the audience he wanted to bring up to the stage to dance with him, Bono spent several minutes trying to get the people to work their way through the crowd and security. When he finally got two fans onto the stage, the three danced together briefly before the band wrapped up the song. The normally six-minute-long "Bad" had gone on for a quarter of an hour. U2 had to leave the stage after just two songs, but once again a live televised performance in front of a massive audience proved to be enormously beneficial for U2.

The appeal of Bono's performance was soon evident. Just prior to Live Aid, the band had released another live minirecording

U2's performance at Live Aid in 1985 gave the band worldwide exposure. Requests for their music at radio stations soared after their appearance.

Cause Concerts and Collaborations

Some people regard the 1980s as a time when rock music became apolitical and apathetic. While it is true that the 1960s were replete with rock protest songs, and the 1970s saw major concert events staged for humanitarian and political causes, such as the Concert for Bangladesh and the No-Nukes Concert, there were also many concerts and recording collaborations for special social and political causes in the 1980s.

U2 donated all the proceeds from an abbreviated U.S. tour in 1984 to the international human rights group Amnesty International. The trend of musicians acting on behalf of causes greatly accelerated when Bob Geldof, an Irish rock star who gained fame with his band the Boomtown Rats, organized a recording session with many British and Irish music stars to produce an album, which included the song "Do They Know It's Christmas?" Geldof and the members of U2 knew each other from Dublin, and Bono and Adam Clayton both appeared on the record. All proceeds from the record went to aid famine victims in Ethiopia. This collaboration inspired Quincy Jones to put together a similar project in the United States, a collaboration of artists called USA for Africa, which produced the song "We Are the World." Geldof was also the mastermind behind the Live Aid show in 1985, a show that proved so important to U2 during their rise to stardom. That same year, Bono collaborated with artists brought together by Bruce Springsteen guitarist Little Steven to make a record protesting South Africa's policy of racial discrimination known as apartheid. Although U2 would not participate in all of them, a number of concert events would take place during the following years to raise consciousness about apartheid.

The following year U2 headlined Amnesty International Concerts that were geared not so much toward raising money but for increasing membership for the organization. The concerts were successful, helping to double the number of U.S. members to seventy thousand. Prior to these appearances, U2 had also headlined a concert in Ireland called Self Aid, which was meant to provide assistance for the large number of young unemployed people in that country.

U2 continued their socially conscientious ways into the 1990s. In 1992, they played a concert for the environmental group Greenpeace, and also made an appearance at a 1997 concert to promote freedom for the people of Tibet. Bono collaborated with rap performer Wyclef Jean at a show in 1999 that was broadcast live on international television and over the Internet as part of Net Aid, an event that took place in three venues simultaneously and was intended to raise funds to fight poverty worldwide.

entitled *Wide Awake in America*. It included four songs, two from *The Unforgettable Fire* and two songs written and recorded for the album but not used. One of the songs included on the record was "Bad." This live version had been surprisingly well received by rock radio stations prior to Live Aid, but after U2's performance, demand for the song skyrocketed, making it one of the most frequently played rock tracks nationwide. Bob Catania, a promoter with U2's label, stressed how important the song was for U2's fortunes. "I'm convinced it was the song that broke them—it made U2 happen." [52]

Backing Words with Actions

Aside from performing for various sociopolitical causes, Bono began to help people victimized by hardship. During 1985, Bono and his wife Ali traveled where many people would likely hesitate to go under the circumstances. They followed up Bono's Live Aid performance by volunteering to serve famine victims in Ethiopia. They helped prepare and hand out meals to starving people. In *Bono: The Biography,* Jackson claims that the trip was motivated largely by conflicted feelings Bono had toward the fame and wealth he was able to enjoy after the band's Live Aid performance. The purpose of that show had been to assist those living in extreme poverty and despair, and Bono worried that the great benefits coming to U2 would undermine their credibility and distract them from their professional and creative goals. "It was to regain his own personal focus that he went to Ethiopia," says Jackson. "He also had a strong need to see the situation out there for himself, and to offer practical help in the famine relief effort." [53]

Bono and Ali spent a full month there, but did so discreetly. The media only discovered their journey toward the end of their stay, and even then the couple remained low-key. This represented Bono's biggest personal charitable act to date, and clearly indicated that he was sincere about the causes he publicly advocated and supported with his performances. During an interview with Larry King on CNN, Bono spoke about his experiences in Ethiopia at that time.

> My life changed. . . . I saw things you shouldn't ever see. . . . We used to get up in the morning . . . as the mist would

lift, you know, over the hills, you would see tens of thousands of people who had been walking all night to get food who were coming to this camp. And sometimes they would leave their children there, and we would get to those children, and the children would be dead.[54]

Bono and Ali would later tell of their experiences in Africa in a photographic exhibition entitled *A String of Pearls* that showed in Dublin in 1988.

Culminating Concert

In 1986, Bono returned to live performing. U2 headlined a tour on behalf of Amnesty International, playing sports arenas and stadiums throughout the United States. Like similar festivals, it featured several leading artists including Sting, Peter Gabriel, and Bryan Adams. During the final night of the tour, Sting reunited with his former group the Police to play a final farewell concert. The concert was held at Giants Stadium outside New York City and was

Bono and Sting answer questions at a news conference for the Amnesty International tour. U2 headlined the tour, which featured some of the biggest bands in rock.

broadcast live for a large television audience. Disagreement ensued over which band should close the show, but as Flanagan recounts, a compromise solution was reached that resulted in a performance that demonstrated that U2 had ascended to a position of supremacy in rock music:

> The great compromise was that U2 got off the stage in time for the Police to have a good chunk of prime television time ... and at the finale of the Police's (excellent) set they went into "Invisible Sun," their haunting song about the troubles in Northern Ireland. One by one the members of U2 emerged from the wings and took over the Police's instruments. . . . Bono stepped up to finish singing the Police's song. It was a graceful gesture, the outgoing Biggest Band in the World publicly handing off the baton to the new one.[55]

An All-Time Great

Yet even then U2 lacked credentials that could be claimed by other top-tier stars of the eighties. For all the growth Bono and the others had experienced as songwriters and performers, and the popularity they had achieved, they still had not reached the Top 10 with a single or an album in the United States. This, however, changed dramatically with the release of their fifth full-length album, *The Joshua Tree,* in 1987. U2 attained record sale levels that put them on a par with the most popular musical artists of the time. The corresponding global concert tour sold out the largest arenas, and observers and critics were overwhelmingly positive in response to the album.

Both *The Joshua Tree* itself and the first two singles from the album reached No. 1 in the United States. U2 also topped the single and album charts in many other countries following *The Joshua Tree*'s release. The album became the fastest-selling album in U.S. history and also the first album to attain platinum status as a compact disc. It sold over 16 million copies worldwide, was named Album of the Year at the Grammy awards in 1988, and in a VH1 poll conducted in 2001 among a quarter-million people it was

The members of U2 pose with their Grammy award for The Joshua Tree *in 1988.* The Joshua Tree *became the fastest-selling album in U.S. history.*

named the greatest album of all time. Among the venues U2 sold out on the tour they headlined to support the album were football stadiums, such as Giants Stadium.

The growth and development that the band had demonstrated on *The Unforgettable Fire* was reflected on *The Joshua Tree.* Influences from many varied forms of music—blues, gospel, and country— could be clearly discerned, and Bono's lyrics also covered deeper and more greatly varied subject matters. "With or Without You" and "Where the Streets Have No Name" both dealt with personal romantic relationships, but unlike most pop love songs, focused on the complexities and challenges of those relationships. "Running to Stand Still" took up where "Bad" from the previous album had left off, dealing with the trauma and destruction of hard drug abuse and addiction. "I Still Haven't Found What I'm Looking For" embodied all the spiritual Christian history and devotion of the band in a joyous, melodic song that became one of the two No. 1 U.S. singles from the album. A particularly poignant song was "One Tree Hill," written in memory of Greg Carroll, a New Zealander who had become a friend of the band and had been working for Bono in Dublin when he was killed in a motorcycle accident. In his 1987 *Rolling Stone* interview, Bono commented on how strongly affected he was by Carroll's death: "It was a devastating blow. He was doing me a favor, he was taking my bike home. . . . He was a best friend."[56] Bono went so far as to compare his reaction to the feelings he experienced after his mother's death.

Media reviews of *The Joshua Tree* were almost totally as positive as this one, which was written by Robert Hillburn in the *Los Angeles Times:* "U2 fills in the sketches with sometimes breathtaking signs of growth. The music . . . is more tailored and assured. . . . [Bono's] lyrics are also more consistently focused and eloquently designed than in past albums, and his singing underscores the band's expressions of disillusionment and hope with new-found power and passion."[57] Media coverage of U2 reached new levels at this time, as they became only the third rock band, after the Beatles and the Who, to appear on the cover of *Time* magazine.

Ongoing Political Commitments

In addition to exploring personal and spiritual issues, *The Joshua Tree* also made the kind of political statements for which U2 had become well known. The song "Mothers of the Disappeared" addressed the issue of abductions and disappearances of political activists at the hands of government agents in Latin America. During a concert performance in Chile, which was televised live throughout that nation, Bono brought actual mothers of vanished government opponents onto the stage during that song and openly appealed for the government to reveal what had become of the women's children. "Bullet the Blue Sky" was inspired by a visit to Central America that Bono and Ali had made in the summer of 1986. Bono and Ali visited Nicaragua and El Salvador, two countries decimated by fierce civil wars. The song featured pointedly disturbing images of war and its aftermath.

With U2's heightened stardom, songs and performances like these greatly elevated their status as political activists and advocates, something that has remained an integral part of their public identities. This was especially true about Bono, and the increased exposure and prominence he experienced proved to be life-changing.

Chapter 4

Sincerity and Showmanship

THE ATTENTION THAT U2's social and political beliefs and activities received gave them status as one of the most relevant musical artists of the time, as well as one of the most popular and creative. This huge fame especially affected Bono, as the most visible band member. At first he struggled with his new public identity and the conflicts and contradictions between his public and private selves. As time went on, he came to terms with the challenges faced by a person of his stature. Bono's reactions to his new status would also dramatically affect the artistic direction in which he would lead U2.

Identity Struggle

There were some indications that Bono was having a hard time adjusting to the level of fame that he had reached. Personality conflicts and complexities that had previously received little attention were now the subject of major media coverage. In the international newspaper the *Christian Science Monitor,* writer Amy Duncan discussed what she saw as inconsistencies between U2's recordings and live performances, and attributed them chiefly to Bono. While describing his live performance at a Madison Square Garden concert as "charming, personable, even intimate," she contrasted this with his compositions on *The Joshua Tree,* describing them as "mostly dark images . . . political oppression, religious questioning, agonizing relationships, war, and hypocrisy."[58]

In fact, Bono was genuine and sincere both in writing meaningful lyrics and in wanting to connect with his live audiences and create excitement and enjoyment during U2's concerts. He had exhibited both these traits throughout U2's existence, but entertainment media people, who were used to dealing with celebrities who deliberately packaged themselves for public consumption, often reacted to Bono's straightforward approach with skepticism and misunderstanding.

Bono struggled at first to adjust to his celebrity status. Eventually, however, he succeeded in reconciling his private personality with his role as rock star.

Bono himself expressed discomfort with his role as a leading music star around this time. He confirmed to David Fricke in a *Rolling Stone* interview that he felt "socially inept," and said he did not think he fit the role he found himself in: "I don't feel like a pop star, and I don't think I look like one."[59] Bono would eventually find a way to reconcile his high public profile with his private personality, but this conflict would be a challenge for some time to come.

Bono's Big Night at the Grammys

As of 2003, U2 had won fifteen Grammy awards, but for Bono, the most memorable Grammy awards ceremony may always be the one held on March 1, 1994. Bono made two appearances at the podium that night, and both ended with controversy.

When U2's *Zooropa* was named Best Alternative Music Album, Bono was the sole representative of the group present to accept the award. In wrapping up his speech, Bono set off a firestorm by using the word generally considered to be the worst expletive in the English language: "I'd like to give a message to the young people of America. And that is: 'We shall continue to abuse our position and f[***] up the mainstream.'" Bono's language caused a major stir, and the network carrying the broadcast was immediately swamped with complaints.

Later that night, Bono had the chance to redeem himself. He gave the introduction for Frank Sinatra when Sinatra was presented with a lifetime achievement award. Bono and Sinatra had become friendly with each other since they had first met in 1987. On this night, Bono paid tribute to the legendary singer: "Rock 'n' roll people love Frank Sinatra because Frank Sinatra has got what we want: swagger and attitude. He's big on attitude. Serious attitude." Bono continued praising Sinatra, and when Sinatra came on stage to take his award he was clearly moved by Bono's introduction, saying, "That's the best welcome I ever had."

Alas, more trouble was to come. After Sinatra had spoken for a few minutes, interlude music suddenly interrupted him and the television broadcast cut to a commercial. Public and media outrage to this— perhaps the greatest singer of all time being kept from speaking on a night he was being honored—was even more intense than it was to Bono's profanity. As Carter Alan put it in *U2: The Road to Pop*, "If anything, Bono's *f*-word comment . . . evened the score a bit with the television execs."

Disappointment and Backlash

Other adversity was looming in Bono's life. During a second U.S. leg of their world tour in 1987, they filmed various concert performances to be included in a forthcoming movie. However, unlike the early 1980s video *Under a Blood Red Sky,* this was not intended to be a straightforward concert video. As Carter Alan put it, the new film, to be titled *Rattle and Hum,* "would document U2's continued search as it toured through the birthplace of blues, gospel, soul, country and western, and rock and roll." [60] Released in late 1988, *Rattle and Hum* turned out to be part documentary, part concert movie. It was accompanied by a two record (in vinyl format) album with the same name. Like U2's previous album, it sold over 10 million copies worldwide and spawned multiple hit singles.

While sales for the *Rattle and Hum* record were strong, attendance for the movie was decidedly disappointing. It lasted only about three weeks in nationwide release in the United States. Further, reviews for both the movie and record were largely negative. *Rolling Stone* said "what really undercuts the project is a lack of focus," and "this is a mess with a mission." [61] The New York City publication the *Village Voice* was even harsher: "By almost any rock 'n' roll fan's standards, U2's *Rattle and Hum* is an awful record." [62] While artists with strong record sales often can and do disregard negative critical reviews, much of U2's strength had been based upon the support they received from those who took rock music most seriously. Their image as a leading creative and relevant band was undermined by negative media attention such as this.

Bono's image was also hurt by his new association with high-level celebrities. Bono and the other band members attended a Hollywood show business gala at the home of Jane Fonda, which included guests like Eddie Van Halen, Valerie Bertinelli, David Crosby, Graham Nash, Charlie Sheen, Charlotte Lewis, Martin Sheen, Oliver Stone, and Julianne Phillips Springsteen. Surrounding himself with these kinds of glamorous personalities seemed to run counter to the sincerity and down-to-earth attitude Bono had conveyed previously in his career.

What incurred even more negative reaction was the parade of big names involved in the making of the *Rattle and Hum* album. There were appearances by Bob Dylan, Lou Reed, and B.B. King. In addition, U2 played cover versions of a Bob Dylan song and "Helter Skelter" by the Beatles, as well as tribute songs to former Beatle John Lennon and legendary jazz-blues singer Billie Holiday. To many, it seemed U2 were acting presumptuously, associating themselves with musical greats who had stood the test of time when they had only recently gained superstar status. Referring to Charles Manson's claims that "Helter Skelter" inspired him to murderous actions, Bono introduced the song by saying, "This is a song that Charles Manson stole from the Beatles, we're stealing it back." Whatever the intention of that statement, *Rolling Stone* writer Steve Pond pointed out that it sounded to many people that "U2 is announcing itself as the heir to the Beatles." [63]

Other statements made by Bono on *Rattle and Hum* further annoyed and alienated many listeners. During two songs in particular, Bono came across as heavy-handed in condemning racism in South Africa and U.S. military policy in Central America. Most troublesome for Bono was a statement he made not on the record but in the *Rattle and Hum* movie. During "Sunday Bloody Sunday," Bono was explicitly contemptuous of the Irish revolutionaries who were fighting against British forces occupying Northern Ireland. "What's the glory in taking a man from his bed and gunning him down in front of his wife and children? Where's the glory in that? Where's the glory in bombing a Remembrance Day parade of old-age pensioners, their medals taken out and polished up for the day? Where's the glory in that?" [64] Bono had previously condemned violence on both sides of the Irish conflict before, but the publicity this especially strong statement received meant that Bono had to be on guard against attack by militants in his homeland.

Complicated Family Life

Bono's public activities and persona were also impacting upon his family life. For the most part, Bono had refrained from speaking about his marriage in public, but he did occasionally discuss his relationship with Ali. In a 1987 *Time* article titled "Band on the

Bono poses with Mick Jagger at the MTV awards in 1999. Associating with big-name celebrities early in his career tarnished Bono's down-to-earth image.

Run," Bono commented on how hard it was to find time to be together with his wife. "When I am away, I'm not at home. When I'm home, I'm not at home. I come in when she is going out." He also commented on Ali's independence and fierce spirit that made her willing to confront head-on the strong-willed Bono: "She will not be worn like a brooch. We have a stormy relationship because she is her own woman."[65]

Bono also expressed mixed feelings about parenthood around this time. He claimed he was "both frightened and excited" by the prospect, but also said that, although he thought Ali would be a good parent, "I feel just too irresponsible."[66] However, on Bono's twenty-ninth birthday in 1989, Ali would give birth to their first child, a daughter named Jordan. Another daughter, Memphis Eve, was born just a little over two years after Jordan, in July 1991. During this period, Bono's schedule remained frenetic and his time away from home very extensive. The conflict between his attachment and sense of obligation to his family and the extraneous demands of being a world-famous superstar weighed more heavily upon Bono as his family grew.

A Critical Crossroads

U2 supported *Rattle and Hum* with what was called the Lovetown tour. The tour visited Europe and Australia, but not the United States, where U2 were now facing serious image problems. The heavy media coverage of Bono, his frequent evocations of various

Balancing a sense of obligation to his family with the demands of being a superstar was very difficult for Bono.

social and political causes, and a sometimes-righteous air combined to create an impression of pompousness. Flanagan recounted a music industry joke that was circulating at the time: "'How many members of U2 does it take to change a lightbulb? Just one: Bono holds the lightbulb and the world revolves around him.'"[67]

Just the frequency with which U2 was being seen and heard in the late 1980s was enough to cause public relations problems. With the release of two full-length albums in less than two years, extensive touring throughout the country, and the release of the *Rattle and Hum* film, U2 had saturated the media. It was a recognition of this overexposure that led U2's management to pass over the United States during the Lovetown tour. However, while in Australia, it became clear that American fans were not the only ones growing tired of the path U2 was taking. Before the show one night, Larry Mullen told Bono that he was growing dissatisfied. After more than two years without a sustained break in touring and recording, burnout seemed to become a problem for the entire band. According to Flanagan, "They became so bored . . . one night they went out and played the whole set backward—and it didn't seem to make any difference."[68]

On New Year's Eve 1989, U2 played the last night of their tour in their hometown of Dublin. It seemed that U2 may have reached the end when Bono told the audience, "We won't see you for a while, we have to go away and dream it all up again."[69] Although the band would keep playing together, and Bono's vision and creativity would play a major role in their future success, it would be a struggle before U2 would once again emerge strong and vibrant.

Battling in Berlin

At Bono's behest, U2 traveled to Berlin in early 1990 to do some work on their next album. Brian Eno's partner, Daniel Lanois, had taken over primary production duties on *The Joshua Tree* and was again working with them on this album. At this time, many historical events were unfolding in Berlin: The Cold War was coming to an end, the forty-five-year-old Berlin Wall was coming down, and the German city was undergoing the beginnings of reunification. Bono thought being in Berlin while this was going on would provide inspiration for the band.

In fact, mishaps beset Bono and the others after their arrival. First they joined a parade of people they thought were marching to the wall to celebrate its coming down, only to discover that the group they had joined, which seemed unexplainably downcast and subdued, were in fact not celebrating the collapsing of the Berlin Wall, but protesting *against* it. Bono was afraid of the repercussions, saying, "Oh, this will make a great headline, 'U2 arrives in West Berlin to protest the pulling down of the Wall.'"[70] Bono also woke one morning to discover that the house he had been put up in had earlier belonged to a family of East Berliners who were visiting the western city in 1961 when the wall went up and were unable to return home. Now, nearly thirty years later, the family had returned to reclaim their house. When they arrived and discovered Bono, they demanded he leave the premises even though he was just waking, and wearing nothing but a T-shirt.

Things were not going well in the recording studio either. A contentious disagreement had developed between Bono and the Edge on one hand, and Clayton, Mullen, and producer Daniel Lanois on the other. Bono and the Edge wanted to incorporate new experimental sounds into U2's music and try to emulate some emerging artists who were employing industrial and techno characteristics into their music. Mullen and Clayton believed the band needed to stay true to the standard rock music parameters they had established for themselves. So severe did the disagreement become that Flanagan, in *U2 at the End of the World*, claims that it even threatened to break up the band: "It has never been this hard for U2 before. The band members begin to consider that they really have reached the end of the line together, that *Rattle and Hum* was the start of a downhill slide they'd best be off halting before it goes any further."[71]

Guidance from an Outside Party

Just as Paul McGuiness intervened to help keep the band together during their conflict over Christianity, another outside party now played a critical role in ensuring the band's future. That was Brian Eno, who was still close with both the band members and Lanois. Flanagan described Eno's role as mediating between the rival factions and convincing them that their differing ideas were not mu-

Disagreements over musical style during the recording of Achtung Baby *threatened to tear the band apart. But the band reconciled their differences and produced a commercially successful album.*

tually exclusive, that they could stay genuine and still explore new sonic territory. After Eno's encouragement, things did take a turn for the better. Flanagan described a composing session that resulted in one of U2's most renowned songs:

> Edge [enters] the studio and starts playing. . . . Larry and Adam fall in behind him on the drums and base. . . . Bono goes out to the microphone and begins improvising words and a melody: "We're one, but we're not the same—we get to carry each other, carry each other."

> U2 plays the new song for about ten minutes. "Is it getting better," Bono sings, "or do you feel the same? Is it any easier on you now that you've got someone to blame?" Edge

feels that it's suddenly all jelling—the band is clicking and all four of them know. They come back into the booth and listen to a playback with a relief close to joy. By the next morning they have recorded "One," as strong a song as U2 has ever written. It came to them all together and it came easily, as a gift. [72]

"One" eventually became a Top 10 hit in both the United States and Britain, and would also earn the distinction of ranking as one of the ten most influential records of all time in a *Rolling Stone*/MTV poll taken at the end of the twentieth century. It was actually similar in sound to earlier U2 songs, but most of the album was markedly different from earlier U2 work. With the new album's release in late 1991, it became clear that the wishes of Bono and the Edge regarding what direction U2 should take had ultimately weighed most heavily on the creation of the new album.

Achtung Baby

Even the name of the new album indicated that U2 had undergone a change. Having always tried to be serious and straightforward in the past, the band now entitled their latest album *Achtung Baby*. The name was adapted from a line of dialogue in the Mel Brooks comedy movie *The Producers*. The techno-industrial sounds Bono and the Edge wanted to use on the new album were strongly pronounced. Thematically, the music also reflected Bono's and the Edge's lives more than the other members of the band, because of their married status. The temptation of glittery nightlife and how it can lure someone away from the security and comfort of one's home and family comprised the subject matter of most of the songs.

Achtung Baby quickly rose on the British and U.S. album charts, and became the third-straight U2 album to sell over 10 million copies. It also received high reviews. Once again, Bono's creative inclinations had been beneficial for the band. *USA Today* described it as "one of the year's best albums. . . . Sonically and lyrically, *Achtung* signals a major departure and growth spurt." [73]

If fans and critics were surprised by U2's new album, they would be even more surprised by what they would see the next time they played live, as Bono's creative vision would also transform U2's stage presentation, especially his own personal performance.

Making a Techno Wonderland

The stage set for the tour accompanying the new album, called Zoo TV during its opening American leg, was a massive collage of large-scale visual effects that centered around giant video screens on the stage. The images on the screens were a combination of live shots from the show, with various graphic images produced for accompaniment and effect. Using handheld remote controls, Bono played live TV broadcasts on the giant screens for the audience.

U2 completely transformed their stage presentation in the 1990s. The band incorporated large-scale visual effects and huge video screens in their performances.

During breaks between songs, he would comment on the snippets that came over the telecast. Later, the tour began playing outdoor stadiums, and the equipment was expanded to include even more and bigger video monitors, four video walls alongside the band's performance space, and several television receiving towers reaching over one hundred feet in the air. The towers even required aircraft warning lights. Each show used twelve hundred tons of equipment, including 176 speaker cabinets and a million watts of power. Carter Alan commented, "Few concert productions were ever this large and none so technologically driven."[74]

Bono commented on the significance of U2's massive-scale concert apparatus in an article appearing in the *Chicago Sun-Times:*

> I love it when rock 'n' roll goes completely out of control. . . . And, forgive the cliché, but you're riding away and the wave gathers speed and you come off your board, you know, that's part of the dilemma—you go back to catch another wave and ride it. This ridiculous, over-the-top exercise is our attempt to show we are actually not running away from the size rock 'n' roll has become, but we're actually kind of taking it on. And now as we get used to it, taking it on with some humor, subverting it somewhat.[75]

Along with the enormity of the stage set, there was another drastic difference in U2's concert performance—Bono's stage presence and presentation.

Costume Chameleon

Throughout his career, Bono had dressed in a straightforward, casual style for his live performances. That ended with this tour. Bono now emerged onstage in full costume, makeup, and in character role. A persona known as "the Fly" would rise up on stage in shadow form, dancing and puffing on a small cigar as the lights rose. (Bono claimed he did not inhale the smoke, but he did struggle with an on-and-off smoking habit starting with these character performances.) Bono's hair was slick and he was clad in black leather. The accessory that was to be of the most lasting significance was a set of dark shades that would become inextricably linked to Bono's image from then on. Later in the show he would

With the 1991 tour, Bono began wearing outrageous costumes on stage like this one.

transform into the Mirrorball Man, wearing a reflective silver suit and mockingly adoring himself in a mirror. In the worldwide tour, Bono would adopt another character, MacPhisto, a Satanlike character with horns, heavily plastered makeup, and a gold lamé jacket.

Bono's satirical, dramatic characters were another way in which he was taking on the image consciousness he had found to be unavoidable in show business. Bono even often stayed in character offstage, especially when he would make promotional appearances or knew he was likely to be spotted by a large number of passersby.

In a 1993 *Rolling Stone* interview, Bono explained his motivations for his character adaptation:

> There were reports of egomania, and I just decided to be-come everything they said I was. Might as well. . . .
>
> I felt like I didn't recognize the person I was supposed to be, as far as what you saw in the media. There's some kind of rape that happens when you are in the spotlight, and you go along with it. . . .
>
> I used to think that if you just had enough time you could get it right. You could just say, "Well, this isn't true, no, no, that isn't so." But this machine is so hungry that you can't. You can just feed it. So what we're doing is like misinfor-mation. [76]

Bono's new approach seemed to have led U2 to greatly renewed success. They had come out of a turbulent period and reemerged as the biggest rock band in the world, and this success appeared to have given Bono and the other band members powerful moti-vation to continue working together.

Creativity Burst

Just how reinvigorated the band was became clear during a four-month touring hiatus between their U.S. concert tours in the fall of 1992 and European stadium dates beginning the following spring. It was widely expected that they would record a few songs for a mini-length record and release it close on the heels of their last full-length album, much as they had done with their live EPs following *War* and *The Unforgettable Fire*. Instead, the band, in an extraordi-nary burst of creativity, produced another full-length album during the brief time. It was titled *Zooropa*, which became the name of the European leg of the tour.

The technological influences that were powerfully present on *Achtung Baby* were even more dominant on *Zooropa*. Heavy electronic rhythms and overdubs drove all but a few of the songs. Bono yielded lead vocals on two distinctive songs: to the Edge on "Numb" and to country-and-western superstar Johnny Cash on "The Wanderer." Like most previous U2 albums, *Zooropa* became a multimillion-

Does Johnny Cash Speak for Bono?

Country music star Johnny Cash was among the many musicians and singers U2 collaborated with starting around the time they produced the *Rattle and Hum* album and movie. His collaboration with U2 actually took place after the band had tried to distance themselves from the *Rattle and Hum* phase of their career. In 1993, Cash became the first nonmember of U2 to have a lead vocal on one of the group's songs when he sang "The Wanderer," the closing track on the album *Zooropa*.

The song is widely considered to be one of the most personally revealing Bono has written, coming off as an attempt to find virtue in being a world traveler and living an extravagant lifestyle while leaving a loving and loyal family behind. In a *Rolling Stone* review of *Zooropa* included in *U2: The Rolling Stone Files,* Anthony DeCurtis describes how Cash's performance fits into the overall album in conveying important aspects of Bono's life experiences:

> Speak-singing with all the moral authority of an Old Testament prophet, Cash serves as a link to a lost world of moral surety ("I went out walking with a bible and a gun/The word of God lay heavy on my heart/I was sure I was the one/Now Jesus, don't you wait up/Jesus, I'll be home soon") literally replacing the various corrupted and confused personas Bono . . . had occupied in the course of the album.

Bill Flanagan also discusses "The Wanderer" in *U2 at the End of the World,* drawing close parallels between the song and Bono's personal life:

> "The Wanderer" . . . seems like a public confession that beneath the fly shades [Bono] is hoping to find God by searching through the glitter and trash.

> The character in the song has used Jesus' exhortation to leave your wife and children and follow Him as an excuse to skip out on his responsibilities. He is playing with the . . . heresy that you can sin your way to salvation ("I went out there in search of experience/To taste and to touch and to feel as much as a man can before he repents.")

selling album, but few songs were radio friendly, and there were no big hit singles. Critical reaction was mixed, as was incisively portrayed by a *Newsweek* review describing the album as "a few great songs and some off-the-cuff studio noodling."[77] Impressively, the band managed to work the new songs into their live set through Europe and the Pacific, even though they had no time to rehearse them between completing their recording and starting their European concert dates.

Addressing Family Issues

The time between the North American and European legs of the tour was a testing period for Bono and Ali's marriage. Those who were close to the couple were especially concerned. The Edge and his wife Aislinn had just separated, and many of Bono and Ali's friends and family feared that the strain of being in U2 could also take a toll on the Hewsons. Adding to that pressure, Ali, who had completed political science studies at a Dublin university, was now getting involved in her own pursuits. She was planning to take an extended trip to Chernobyl, the site of the world's worst nuclear power accident, to help relief efforts and work on a documentary film.

Although Bono had been on the road with U2 for almost eight months, Ali was reluctant to let him come back with the family right away, and suggested he consider staying in a hotel his first week back in Dublin. "I don't want to, but Ali says it's better," Bono told Bill Flanagan. "A couple of days after I get back to Dublin we've got to be on a TV special. It will just confuse the kids if I come home and start working again right away, and she says they'll be hurt if they talk to me and I don't hear them." [78] However, Bono did move right back in with Ali when he returned to Dublin. He also made greater efforts to devote time to his family, bringing his daughter Jordan to a recording session, and missing important mixing and production sessions to stay home during the week before Ali left for Chernobyl. With his actions, Bono began solidifying his relationship with his family. Strong professional success with U2 and growing closeness with his family would both continue for Bono throughout the 1990s and beyond.

Chapter 5

Where No Rock Star Has Gone Before

Durinng the 1990s, several aspects of Bono's professional and personal life that had previously been unsettling for him showed signs of stabilizing. Benefiting from continued musical success and strengthened family ties, Bono embarked upon a great variety of creative and political activities that further raised his profile and earned him greater esteem as both an artist and humanitarian activist. While U2 would continue to be Bono's principal creative outlet, he would also over the next several years pursue several other creative endeavors both on his own and with others outside of the group.

Remaining Relevant

Although it was not so readily apparent, U2's new music and stage shows still contained political expressions. Part of their touring apparatus consisted of hollowed out, psychedelically painted Trabant cars. Trabants were a product of the now defunct East Germany. With demand for Trabants virtually wiped out, U2 purchased several for their concerts, and used them for visual effects, hanging them from the ceilings and placing spotlights inside them. This symbolization of the collapse of the Iron Curtain and the resolution of the Cold War was offset by other images and statements that were not so positive.

Antiwar feelings remained strong among members of U2, including opposition to the war in the Persian Gulf against Iraq that had been fought by a U.S.-led coalition in 1991. In addition to

Bono speaks at the launch of Operation Christmas Child, a humanitarian mission to provide supplies to young AIDS victims worldwide.

including some graphic and powerful war footage during their concerts' video presentations, the band took pointed aim at then U.S. president George Bush. The U.S. shows opened with spliced-together video of Bush giving a televised speech intended to rally support for the Gulf War. In a broken voice and with jerky body motions, Bush seemed to be reciting the anthemic lyrics from the Queen song "We Will Rock You" to the accompaniment of a powerful percussive beat.

In fact, the entire Zoo TV equipment configuration was in itself an outgrowth of a political statement. Flanagan describes the thought processes that evolved between Bono and the Edge as they were watching television news coverage of the Gulf War:

> Edge is struck by the fact that the young pilots returning from bombing raids and the soldiers directing the missiles from launchpads far from Baghdad often compare what

they're doing to playing video games. . . . They never see any blood or destruction. . . . Edge and Bono are watching TV together when a young American pilot is interviewed on CNN. When asked what the bombing looks like from the plane, he says, "It's so realistic." Bono and Edge look at each other, amazed.

Bono thinks that something fundamental has changed, not just in the world's political structure, but in the way media has permeated the public's consciousness. In the last decade cable TV has spread through what used to be called the free world. There is no more line between news, entertainment, and home shopping. Bono says that when U2 tour . . . they have to figure out a way to represent this new reality.[79]

The band also expressed itself politically in more direct ways. Among their activities were promoting voter participation among young people in the United States, joining a large protest against a radioactive waste plant in England, and speaking out against neo-Nazism, which had been on the rise worldwide in the 1980s and early 1990s.

U2's most controversial actions during the European portion of their tour involved live video and telephone hookups with people in Sarajevo, a city in the Balkan country Bosnia-Herzegovina, which at that time was beset by gruesome warfare between rival ethnic factions. The people in Sarajevo related stories of horror, brutality, and deprivation. This was typified by an angry rant delivered one night to an audience in Glasgow, Scotland, by a Bosnian woman: "We would like to hear the music, too, but we only hear the screams of wounded and tortured people and raped women!"[80]

These nightly video conferences from a live war zone had a powerful impact upon the audiences and sometimes even the band members. Often the crowd would become subdued afterward. There was also strong negative reaction from some of the media. The British magazine *New Music Express* said "The Bosnian hookup was beyond bad taste. It was insulting."[81] Yet U2 continued with them through a major four-night stand at London's Wembley Stadium, due largely to Bono's passion and commitment toward the victims of the tragedy in Bosnia.

Bono had become especially riled about Bosnia when two Bosnian representatives spent time on tour with the band in Europe. While Bono had been involved with humanitarian relief efforts for Bosnia, his conversations with the Bosnians convinced him that his efforts were in vain because those in control would not allow relief funds and materials to reach those they were intended for. Bono said he felt like he was only "feeding a graveyard."[82] Frustrated, Bono had initially tried to get U2 to go to Sarajevo to perform in solidarity with the war victims. He had stubbornly persisted in his efforts until finally convinced by one of the Bosnian representatives, who had returned to Sarajevo, that a U2 show in Sarajevo would be too high-risk for too many people. The phone and video hookups were an alternative Bono had settled for, and he was determined to continue using them, at least until he believed the world's attention had been drawn to the tragedy in the Balkans.

U2 finally did play Sarajevo on September 23, 1997, after a peace settlement had been reached and international military troops had secured the area. In *Bono: The Biography,* Jackson portrays how significant the event was for Bono:

> It was an emotional experience for Bono. Earlier in the day he had been greatly moved when a couple of small local children had solemnly handed him a few spent bullets which had been dug out of their bedroom wall. . . . In their innocence, they had bizarrely wrapped them as a present for him.
>
> With the best will in the world, though, the gig . . . did not go smoothly because fairly early on Bono lost his voice.
>
> He was gutted, though, that it should strike on that particular night. As it happened, the generosity and the huge reservoir of goodwill among the crowd was enough to buoy Bono up as the audience sang, hummed, even whistled as best they could, to help out. . . .
>
> Soon after, he declared, "It was one of the toughest and one of the sweetest nights of my life."[83]

Diverse Creative Ventures

While U2 remained Bono's major creative channel, the 1990s also saw him undertaking more ventures on his own. During the 1980s,

Bono visits a bombed-out building in Sarajevo. U2 performed in Sarajevo in 1997 to draw attention to the tragedy of the war in Bosnia.

Bono had worked on a couple of charitable collaborations outside of U2. He had performed on the single "Do They Know It's Christmas?" by Band Aid, an ensemble of major British pop stars organized to help famine victims in Ethiopia. Bono had also sung on another multiartist collaboration called Artists United Against Apartheid (the system of racial discrimination then in effect in South Africa) and, along with the Edge, Bono had also written a song for Roy Orbison, "She's a Mystery to Me," that Orbison included on his last album before his death in 1989.

During the 1990s, Bono sang duets with big-name performers from many different musical backgrounds. These included old-time vocalist Frank Sinatra (Bono also appeared in a music video with Sinatra), opera star Luciano Pavarotti (they sang "Miss Sarajevo," the proceeds from which went to relief efforts for Bosnia), and Haitian rap star Wyclef Jean.

Another major project for Bono in the 1990s was coauthoring a screenplay for a movie entitled *The Million Dollar Hotel*. It was set in a once high-class hotel that had become run-down and was occupied by a strange mix of homeless and vagrant characters. The story centered on a mysterious death at the hotel that led to a murder investigation. Bono first created the screenplay with a friend, movie scriptwriter Nicholas Klein. While staying in Southern California during the Zoo TV tour, Bono actively tried to get the movie produced, and there were many people interested in participating, but personality conflicts among them made things very

U2's Albums

Release Date	Title
October 1980	*Boy*
October 1981	*October*
March 1983	*War*
November 1983	*Under a Blood Red Sky*
October 1984	*The Unforgettable Fire*
May 1985	*Wide Awake in America*
March 1987	*The Joshua Tree*
October 1988	*Rattle and Hum*
November 1991	*Achtung Baby*
July 1993	*Zooropa*
March 1997	*Pop*
March 1998	*Best of 1980–1990*
October 2000	*All That You Can't Leave Behind*
November 2002	*Best of 1990–2000*

Source: www.U2.com.

difficult for Bono. The biggest stumbling block was over who would direct the film. Bono wanted Phil Joanou, who had worked on *Rattle and Hum* and some of U2's music videos. Gary Oldman, the actor Bono wanted for a leading role, also wanted Joanou on the film—in fact, he said he would only appear in it if Joanou directed. However, the film's financial support was being provided by Mel Gibson's production company. Gibson disliked Joanou and did not want him on the film.

Attempting to get his film made, Bono became involved in the power struggles of Hollywood's high and mighty. He arranged a lunch between Joanou and Gibson, hoping to bring about agreement on who would direct, but no one changed positions, and *The Million Dollar Hotel* was shelved. A couple of years later work would resume on the project. German director Wim Wenders would handle the film, and Mel Gibson himself would be the featured actor. The film would not be released until 2000, when it would appear mostly as part of various international film festivals. Its limited release prevented the film from being much of a box-office success. It did receive an award at the Berlin Film Festival, but reviews were largely mixed. It seemed pretty clear that Bono was not going to achieve the same level of recognition for his film work as he did for his music.

New U2 Material

Recognition for Bono's musical achievement would continue to be highly positive with the release of U2's next album, entitled *Pop,* in March 1997. Most of the songs were heavily influenced by techno and club dance music, including the hit single, "Discotheque," and the song "Mofo," on which Bono speaks to his mother, whose loss so strongly affected him more than twenty years before. Critically, the album was widely hailed. Writing in the *Sunday Times* (London), Andrew Smith went so far as to say U2 "have made their first great album. . . . They have taken the spirit of the new electronic music and used it to inspire a fabulous rock album." [84]

In support of *Pop,* U2 would once again undertake an extravaganza of a worldwide concert tour. Dubbed the Pop Mart tour, it exceeded even the Zoo TV/Zooropa tour stage set, supporting the world's largest video screen, at 176-by-60 feet, and thirty tons of sound equipment. Giant visuals onstage included McDonald's-like arches and a cocktail olive, but the most talked-about stage gadget on the tour was a forty-foot-high lemon on a robotic arm that transformed into a mirror ball between the main set and encore. The members of the band would emerge from the device in lavish costumes.

This tour grossed hundreds of millions of dollars worth of ticket sales. Included among the dates was a show in Reggio Emilia, Italy, where U2 played to their biggest crowd ever, about one hundred fifty thousand people. Yet the media and public reaction to the tour was not strong. Many thought that the over-the-top aspect to the shows had become tired, and messages or themes seemed murky and confused. Adam Clayton indicated his own feelings were along these lines: "Whatever we were playing around with, it wasn't touching the right buttons."[85] Ticket prices had risen to very high levels, and in some places sales were disappointing. The last two largely experimental albums had sold well by common standards, but did lag behind earlier U2 blockbusters. Overall enthusiasm for the course U2 had charted during the 1990s seemed to be subsiding.

The Family Grows

In the few years leading up to the release of *Pop,* Bono had spent more time with his family. After the release of her Chernobyl documentary, Ali had once again largely kept out of the public eye, although she continued to be active in efforts to aid Chernobyl victims. Family time together included Ali and their two daughters accompanying Bono on the road for part of the Pop Mart tour. That the bond among the family had grown stronger was further confirmed by the birth of two more children over the next few years, both of them sons. Elijah was born on August 11, 1999, and John Abraham on May 20, 2001. In an interview with Larry King on CNN, Bono commented on how being a parent affected him and his outlook on the world:

> People . . . probably thought having children would chill me out. Rather the opposite. It's made me a lot more interested in the world, the way it's shaped and formed, the world they're about to enter into. And it's made me more interested in politics for that reason, and less patient with the process of politics, in sort of correcting the mistakes we've made [during the past].[86]

Bono's son, Elijah, was born in August 1999. Being a father has made Bono more interested in taking an active role in a variety of social and political causes.

Expanding Activism

Perhaps it was this increased level of consciousness that led Bono to step up his political and humanitarian efforts even more. He and the other band members actively supported a peace agreement for Northern Ireland that was reached in April 1998. The agreement needed to be voted on in both Ireland and Northern Ireland, and

Bono and the Bushes

Over the course of several years, Bono has had an interesting relationship with both of the George Bushes who have served as U.S. presidents. During the 1992 Zoo TV tour, the first President Bush was satirically targeted in U2's stage show. Bush was shown in a heavily edited segment on the giant video cameras giving a speech in which he appears to be chanting lyrics from the Queen song "We Will Rock You." Bono also tried to phone Bush on many occasions from the concert stage. These kinds of prank calls were a part of U2's concerts every night on the tour. During the U.S. concerts, more often than not, it would be the White House that Bono would ring up.

Bono never got past the switchboard operators, and in appreciation for their putting up with him he offered them free passes to U2's concert when they played in Washington, D.C. The first president Bush, however, was apparently still irate over U2's treatment of him. At the time, Bush was running for reelection against Bill Clinton, and Clinton had met with the members of U2 to sound them out on the global issues they considered important. At one campaign stop, Bush made this statement:

> Clinton . . . was in Hollywood seeking foreign policy advice from the rock [group] U2. Now understand I have nothing against U2, you might not know this but they try to call me at the White House every night from their concert. But the next time we face a foreign policy crisis, I will work with [British prime minister] John Major and [Russian president] Boris Yeltsin, and . . . Clinton can consult Boy George [eccentric singer with the group Culture Club]. I'll stick with the experts.

Bush's son, George W. Bush, seems to be of a different mind than his father regarding Bono. Likewise, Bono seems more amenable to the younger Bush than to the elder. The second president Bush met with Bono at the White House in March 2002. Bush had high compliments for the U2 front man in a speech he gave after the meeting, which is posted on the official White House website (www.white house.gov): "He is willing to use his position in a responsible way. He is willing to lead to achieve what his heart tells him, and that is nobody—nobody—should be living in poverty and hopelessness in the world."

For his part, Bono has often said he believes the second president Bush can be fair and reasonable regarding issues such as relieving debt and providing assistance to poor and disease-ravaged nations. While the two have serious political differences, George W. Bush has shown that he at least respects Bono and takes his work on international issues seriously.

to help rally support for the agreement U2 performed a free concert in Belfast. The two main principles in reaching the agreement, John Hume, a Catholic political leader, and David Trimble, a Protestant leader, both were in attendance. Jackson recounts the scene in *Bono: The Biography:*

> The most enduring image of the gig came when Bono asked David Trimble and John Hume up on stage in what would be the veteran politicians' first joint appearance of the referendum campaign. Bono introduced them as two of the architects of the peace agreement, two men willing to leave the past behind in order to forge ahead.
>
> Standing between the pair, Bono . . . simultaneously raised aloft David Trimble's left arm and John Hume's right arm in a salute. And a great cheer rang out. [87]

The peace agreement was ratified by voters in both countries by wide margins, but Bono did not limit his efforts to Irish issues. He had long been aware of how hard it was for impoverished countries to sustain economic growth because of long-term debt obligations they had to more affluent nations. In 1999, Bono became active with Jubilee 2000, an organization that lobbied government leaders in the world's wealthy and powerful nations to forgive debt against poorer nations. In this capacity with Jubilee 2000, later renamed Drop the Debt, Bono would have some of the most high-profile meetings of his life. These would include discussions with two U.S. presidents, Bill Clinton and George W. Bush, British prime minister Tony Blair, United Nations secretary general Kofi Annan, and Pope John Paul II.

His efforts to promote international debt relief also led Bono to actively lobby members of the U.S. Congress and to engage many other government and business leaders. One high-ranking U.S. official who developed a particularly close relationship with Bono was Paul O'Neill, who was U.S. treasury secretary from 2001 to 2002. Initially O'Neill refused to respond to Bono's attempts to meet with him. "I thought he was just some pop star who wanted to use me," said O'Neill. But he had a big change of heart after Bono finally succeeded in getting together with him. "He's a serious person. He cares deeply about these issues, and you know what? He knows a lot about them."[88] Bono and O'Neill made news when they traveled together through Africa in spring 2002 to observe the effects of severe poverty on that continent.

Another cause Bono took up was also of primary concern to Africa. The AIDS epidemic is terribly severe on that continent, and the economic situation makes it very difficult for people to obtain medication to treat the disease. Bono has been prominent in efforts to make AIDS treatment drugs affordable, speaking out against policies that enabled certain drug companies to have monopolies on the markets in African countries. Bono's efforts are credited with helping convince those drug companies to allow less-expensive generic drugs to become available. In early 2001, he also started a new organization in cooperation with Microsoft CEO Bill Gates. Bono explained the organization's name, DATA: "Debt, AIDS and trade for Africa, in return for democracy, accountability and transparency in Africa."[89]

Still Going Strong with U2

Bono's increased political and advocacy activity actually interfered with the recording of the next U2 album, which had begun in spring 1999 but was delayed into the new year. However, the album was

Bono and other members of the humanitarian group Jubilee 2000 met with Pope John Paul II in 2000. Here, in a light moment, the Pope returns Bono's sunglasses after trying them on.

U2's Grammy Awards Through 2001

Year	Category	Title of Work
1987	Best Rock Performance by a Duo or Group with Vocal	The Joshua Tree (Album)
1988	Best Rock Performance by a Duo or Group with Vocal	"Desire" (Single)
1992	Best Rock Performance by a Duo or Group with Vocal	Achtung Baby (Album)
1993	Best Alternative Music Performance	Zooropa (Album)
2000	Best Rock Performance by a Duo or Group with Vocal	"Beautiful Day" (Single)
2000	Song of the Year	"Beautiful Day" (Single)
2000	Record of the Year	"Beautiful Day" (Single)
2001	Best Rock Performance by a Duo or Group with Vocal	"Elevation" (Single)
2001	Best Pop Performance by a Duo or Group with Vocal	"Stuck in a Moment You Can't Get Out Of" (Single)
2001	Best Rock Album	All That You Can't Leave Behind (Album)
2001	Record of the Year	"Walk On" (Single)

Source: www.grammy.com.

overwhelmingly well received by the public and critics when it was finally released in late 2000.

All That You Can't Leave Behind, U2's tenth album of original material, debuted at No. 1 on the album charts in thirty-two countries, including the United States. The first single from the album, "Beautiful Day," released in advance of the album, quickly reached No. 1 in both Britain and the United States, and also won three Grammy awards in 2001, including Song of the Year and Record of the Year. The following year, U2 won four more Grammies for the album or songs from the album, including Best Rock Album and Record of the Year for another single from the album, "Walk On." Like its predecessors, *All That You Can't Leave Behind* went multiplatinum. The review that appeared in *Rolling Stone* was typical of the media reaction to the album. They called it the band's "third masterpiece" and said "the album represents the most uninterrupted collection of strong melodies U2 have ever mounted."[90]

Although the album reflected the entirety of U2's experience, it was definitely marked by a reduction in the electronic and techno influences that characterized the previous few albums.

Mourning a Fellow Lead Singer

On a few occasions, Bono has been moved by the death of someone close to him to write songs about the experience. One such case was the suicide of Michael Hutchence, the lead singer of the Australian rock group INXS, in 1997. His death led to Bono's writing the song "Stuck in a Moment You Can't Get Out Of" on *All That You Can't Leave Behind*.

To a large degree, U2 and INXS had paralleled each other in their rises to success in the 1980s. INXS had not remained as popular into the 1990s, but Hutchence did receive much attention from the British tabloid press, centering largely around his relationship with Paula Yates, the estranged wife of Irish rock star Bob Geldof. It was widely speculated that this intrusive scrutiny into his private life contributed greatly to Hutchence's suicide.

Bono had become friends with Hutchence, and after Paula Yates took her own life, Bono talked openly about conversations he had with Hutchence before his death. The two had actually talked about suicide. "We both agreed how pathetic it was," Bono said in Chris Heath's January 18, 2001, *Rolling Stone* article titled "U2 Band of the Year." Bono believed that if Hutchence had waited just briefly before taking his life he would have gotten past the crisis and not have committed suicide: "If he had lasted half an hour longer, he would be alive now. He couldn't see past, he couldn't see out of that half an hour." Considering the number of times Bono had lost people close to him to untimely death, it is understandable that he would feel bitter over Hutchence's suicide, as he expressed in the same *Rolling Stone* article:

> In the song, I'm right there—it's like, just wanting to be in that half hour. . . . I felt the biggest respect I could pay him was not to write some stupid soppy . . . song, so I wrote a really tough, nasty little number. Sort of, you know, slapping him around the head. And I'm sorry, but that's how it came out for me.

Thematically and topically, the songs covered both personal relationships and issues as well as global political concerns. "Walk On" was written as a tribute to a Burmese political activist, Daw Aung San Suu Kyi, who was being kept under house arrest by that nation's military dictatorship. "Stuck in a Moment You Can't Get Out Of" was a tribute to another band's lead singer, Michael Hutchence of INXS, a friend of Bono's who had committed suicide in 1997. "Kite" was a song about separation and moving on from loved ones, and was especially inspired by Bono's relationships with his children.

When U2 went on the road again, their stage set, like the music on the new album, was also on a much smaller scale than on their previous two tours, although it still included some video screens and other equipment for visual effects. U2 again played to large, sold-out venues all over the world. The great success and acclaim the band received in response to the album and the tour reaffirmed their premier status in the world of music, yet all was not going well with Bono.

Personal and Global Tragedy

In August 2001, Bono announced that his father had terminal cancer. At the time, U2 were touring Europe, and Bono would travel back to Dublin every night after their show by private jet to sleep beside his father in his hospital room. With the strains and conflicts in his relationship with his father now far behind him, Bono dedicated the song "Kite" to his father during U2's concerts. Bob Hewson died later that month. All the band members, Paul McGuiness, Ali, Bono's children, and his brother Norman attended the funeral. The very next day U2 had a major concert scheduled at Slane Castle, a large and famous venue in Dublin. Showing great strength and courage, Bono went ahead with the show. In paying tribute to his father during the concert, Bono confirmed that he was still a man of faith: "I want to thank God for taking my old man away from his sickness and his tired old body and giving him a new one,"[91] he told the crowd.

Even as Bono was recovering from the loss of his father, he and U2 were thrust into a major role in the aftermath of the

September 11, 2001, terrorist attacks against America. Their image as artists whose music conveyed messages of hope and renewal made them a prime choice for inclusion in the special program called *A Tribute to Heroes,* which was put together to aid survivors of the tragedies. U2 was also scheduled to return to the United States the following month for more tour dates. Many other artists were canceling shows following the terrorist attacks, but U2 decided to heed the call of New York mayor Rudolph Giuliani not to submit to fear and to proceed with life as normally as possible. They performed three shows scheduled for Madison Square Garden at the end of October, but did not let the recent horrible events go unacknowledged. During the song "One," they scrolled the names of those lost or missing in the attacks on a video screen behind the stage. This was the same form of tribute they would use during the Super Bowl halftime performance a few months later.

When Bono stood before the Super Bowl crowd at the Superdome in New Orleans and held open his jacket to display an embroidered American flag in the lining, some people saw it as a shift away from political views Bono had taken in the past, such as opposing American military actions in Central America and Iraq. Yet it was in fact consistent with the kinds of aid and comfort Bono had always given to people victimized by hardship and horror of various kinds. When people needed help in dealing with famine, war, political repression, or economic hardship, Bono had been consistently willing to take actions that could make a difference in the lives of those people. Following September 11, Bono offered the American people entertainment to provide comfort and support. Indeed, given his history as both a humanitarian and an entertainer of substance and inspiration, Bono was perhaps uniquely qualified to front the show for halftime at Super Bowl XXXVI.

The Future

Having accomplished so much in his life, Bono, at age forty-three, still most likely has many years ahead of him to further his achievements. When asked by Larry King what he envisioned for himself,

Bono and President George W. Bush appear outside the White House following a discussion of global development in March 2002.

Bono seemed uncertain. "I don't know if I want to be in a rock band in my 60s," Bono said, but nor was he enthusiastic about the prospect of continued political and humanitarian activism. Bono indicated he wished others, particularly those with direct political power, would take up the kinds of causes he did more frequently. "I don't want to do this other job," he said. "It's an accident of fate that I ended up in this place." [92]

Nevertheless, it is an impressive place to have ended up. *Irish Times* writer John Waters reflected upon Bono's associations with high-ranking world leaders and the support and admiration he has received from them:

Bono is now going where no celebrity spokesman for his generation has gone before, earned considerable international respect for himself and his motivations and somehow managed to crack the code of the old conundrum concerning whether rock 'n' roll can move beyond . . . obsession with sex and drugs.[93]

That may be remarkable in itself, but Bono's winning a prestigious human rights award from the Simon Wiesenthal Center and his credible candidacy for a Nobel Peace Prize show that, before he is through, Bono could well go some other places totally unexpected and win even more respect and admiration in the process.

Notes

Introduction: Music with a Message

1. Quoted during a concert performance on December 17, 1981, at the Malibu nightclub in Lido Beach, New York. Recorded and broadcast by radio station WLIR-FM, Garden City, New York. Taped by the author.
2. Quoted in Greg Kot, "Bono's Victory," *Rolling Stone,* December 28, 2000–January 4, 2001, p. 39.
3. Josh Tyrangiel, "Bono," *Time,* March 4, 2002, p. 64.

Chapter 1: Becoming Bono Vox

4. Quoted in Bill Flanagan, *U2 at the End of the World.* New York: Delacorte Press, 1995, p. 525.
5. Quoted in Flanagan, *U2 at the End of the World,* p. 525.
6. Eamon Dunphy, *The Unforgettable Fire: Past, Present, and Future— The Definitive Biography of U2.* New York: Warner Books, 1988, p. 20.
7. Quoted in David Breskin, "Bono: The Rolling Stone Interview," in *U2: The Rolling Stone Files.* New York: Rolling Stone Press, 1994, p. 81.
8. Quoted in Flanagan, *U2 at the End of the World,* p. 315.
9. Dunphy, *The Unforgettable Fire,* p. 13.
10. Dunphy, *The Unforgettable Fire,* p. 25.
11. Quoted in Christopher Connelly, "Keeping the Faith," in *U2: The Rolling Stone Files.* New York: Rolling Stone Press, 1994, p. 32.
12. Connelly, "Keeping the Faith," p. 32.
13. Quoted in Breskin, "Bono: The Rolling Stone Interview," p. 81.

14. Quoted in Connelly, "Keeping the Faith," p. 32.

15. Dunphy, *The Unforgettable Fire,* p. 67.

16. Laura Jackson, *Bono: The Biography.* London: Judy Piatkus, 2001, p. 12.

17. Dunphy, *The Unforgettable Fire,* p. 68.

18. Quoted in Breskin, "Bono: The Rolling Stone Interview," p. 84.

19. Quoted in Jay Cocks, "Band on the Run," *Time,* April 27, 1987, p. 72.

Chapter 2: The Heart and Soul of U2

20. Dunphy, *The Unforgettable Fire,* p. 78.

21. Flanagan, *U2 at the End of the World,* p. 151.

22. Quoted in Breskin, "Bono: The Rolling Stone Interview," p. 83.

23. Bill Graham, "Yep, It's U2," *Hot Press,* January 1, 1978, www.atu2.com.

24. Dunphy, *The Unforgettable Fire,* p. 100.

25. James Henke, "Blessed Are the Peacemakers," in *U2: The Rolling Stone Files.* New York: Rolling Stone Press, 1994, p. 11.

26. Quoted in Henke, "Blessed Are the Peacemakers," p. 11.

27. Quoted in Flanagan, *U2 at the End of the World,* pp. 523–524.

28. Paul Morley, *New Music Express,* October 25, 1980, www.U2.com.

29. "What the Press Said" (Billboard Magazine), February 14, 1981, www.U2.com.

30. Quoted in *Hot Press,* October 1979. www.U2.com.

31. Quoted in Carter Alan, *U2: The Road to Pop.* Boston: Faber and Faber, 1997, pp. 24–25.

32. Quoted in Alan, *U2: The Road to Pop,* p. 20.

33. Quoted in Connelly, "Keeping the Faith," p. 35.

34. Quoted in James Henke, "U2: Here Comes the 'Next Big Thing,'" in *U2: The Rolling Stone Files.* New York: Rolling Stone Press, 1994, p. 1.

35. Dunphy, *The Unforgettable Fire,* p. 167.

36. Dunphy, *The Unforgettable Fire,* p. 171.

37. Quoted in Flanagan, *U2 at the End of the World,* p. 524.

38. Dunphy, *The Unforgettable Fire,* p. 175.

39. Dunphy, *The Unforgettable Fire,* pp. 190–191.

40. Dunphy, *The Unforgettable Fire,* p. 202.

Chapter 3: Gaining Superstardom

41. Quoted in Henke, "Blessed Are the Peacemakers," p. 13.
42. Quoted in Henke, "Blessed Are the Peacemakers," p. 14.
43. Richard Harrington, "When Rock Looks at War; Three New Albums Attack the Issue," *Washington Post,* April 3, 1983, p. C1.
44. Quoted in Connelly, "Keeping the Faith," p. 35.
45. Alan, *U2: The Road to Pop,* pp. 67–68.
46. Quoted in Alan, *U2: The Road to Pop,* p. 73.
47. Quoted in Alan, *U2: The Road to Pop,* p. 74.
48. Quoted in "Random Notes—U2 Live, A Bit Too Much," in *U2: The Rolling Stone Files.* New York: Rolling Stone Press, 1994, p. 17.
49. Kurt Loder, "Unforgettable Fire Album Review," in *U2: The Rolling Stone Files.* New York: Rolling Stone Press, 1994, p. 20.
50. Quoted in Niall Stokes, *U2: Into the Heart: The Stories Behind Every Song.* New York: Thunder's Mouth Press, 2002, p. 54.
51. Connelly, "Keeping the Faith," p. 28.
52. Quoted in Alan, *U2: The Road to Pop,* p. 130.
53. Jackson, *Bono: The Biography,* p. 70.
54. Bono, interview with Larry King, *Larry King Weekend,* CNN, December 1, 2002.
55. Flanagan, *U2 at the End of the World,* p. 92.
56. Quoted in Breskin, "The Rolling Stone Interview, p. 92.
57. Robert Hillburn, "U2's Roots Go Deeper," *Los Angeles Times,* 1987, p. 61, www.U2.com.

Chapter 4: Sincerity and Showmanship

58. Amy Duncan, "U2 Sending Out Mixed Signals to Fans," *Christian Science Monitor,* November 4, 1987, p. 21.
59. Quoted in David Fricke, "Year-End Review of *Rattle and Hum,*" in *U2: The Rolling Stone Files.* New York: Rolling Stone Press, 1994, p. 138.
60. Alan, *U2: The Road to Pop,* p. 187.
61. Quoted in Breskin, "Bono: The Rolling Stone Interview," p. 84.
62. Quoted in Steve Pond, "Now What? Having Conquered the World, U2 Tries to Figure Out What to Do Next," in *U2: The Rolling Stone Files.* New York: Rolling Stone Press, 1994, p. 146.

63. Pond, "Now What? Having Conquered the World, U2 Tries to Figure Out What to Do Next," p. 149.

64. Quoted in Flanagan, *U2 at the End of the World*, p. 370.

65. Quoted in Cocks, "Band on the Run," p. 72.

66. Quoted in Breskin, "Bono: The Rolling Stone Interview," p. 91.

67. Flanagan, *U2 at the End of the World*, p. 5.

68. Flanagan, *U2 at the End of the World*, p. 4.

69. Quoted in Flanagan, *U2 at the End of the World*, p. 4.

70. Quoted in Flanagan, *U2 at the End of the World*, p. 2.

71. Flanagan, *U2 at the End of the World*, pp. 7–8.

72. Flanagan, *U2 at the End of the World*, p. 11.

73. Edna Gundersen, "U2's Probing 'Achtung Baby' Commands Attention," *USA Today*, December 9, 1991, p. 6D.

74. Alan, *U2: The Road to Pop*, p. 226.

75. Quoted in Richard Harrington, "U2 Goes over the Top with Zoo Tour," *Chicago Sun-Times*, September 14, 1992, p. 4.

76. Quoted in Alan Light, "Behind the Fly—Bono: The Rolling Stone Interview," in *U2: The Rolling Stone Files*. New York: Rolling Stone Press, 1994, p. 191.

77. Quoted in Jeff Giles, "U2 Gets Carried Away," *Newsweek*, July 12, 1993, p. 63.

78. Quoted in Flanagan, *U2 at the End of the World*, p. 142.

Chapter 5: Where No Rock Star Has Gone Before

79. Flanagan, *U2 at the End of the World*, p. 13.

80. Quoted in Flanagan, *U2 at the End of the World*, p. 307.

81. Quoted in Flanagan, *U2 at the End of the World*, p. 308.

82. Quoted in Flanagan, *U2 at the End of the World*, p. 285.

83. Quoted in Jackson, *Bono: The Biography*, p. 163.

84. Andrew Smith, "Pop," *Sunday Times* (London), March 23, 1997.

85. Quoted in Jackson, *Bono: The Biography*, p. 159.

86. Bono, interview by Larry King.

87. Jackson, *Bono: The Biography*, pp. 175–176.

88. Quoted in Tyrangiel, "Bono," p. 64.

89. Quoted in "Gates, Bono Unveil 'DATA Agenda' for Africa," February 3, 2002. www.cnn.com.

90. James Hunter, *"All That You Can't Leave Behind* Review," *Rolling Stone,* November 9, 2000, www.rollingstone.com.

91. Quoted in Jackson, *Bono: The Biography,* p. 225.

92. Bono, interview by Larry King.

93. John Waters, "Bono, Going Where No Rock Star Has Gone Before," *Irish Times,* March 4, 2002, p. 14.

Important Dates in the Life of Bono

1960

Bono is born on May 10 to Bob and Iris Hewson in Dublin, Ireland.

1972

Bono attends Mount Temple School.

1974

Bono's mother, Iris Hewson, dies. Bono seeks solace in music and religion.

1976

Bono meets Alison Stewart. Bono joins a band called Feedback, which includes all the people who would ultimately make up U2.

1977

Feedback play a couple of school social events, change their name to the Hype, and start playing small clubs and warm-up gigs in and around the city of Dublin.

1978

The Hype become U2 and the band wins a talent contest with a prize of a recording and distribution contract with CBS Records in Ireland. U2 hire Paul McGuiness as manager.

1979

U2 record first record *U2-3*. U2 play their first live shows in the UK.

1980

U2 land a major recording contract with Island Records. The album *Boy* is recorded and released. U2 tour continental Europe and North America for the first time.

1981

Bono becomes involved with the charismatic Christian group Shalom. U2's second album, *October,* is recorded and released.

1982

Bono marries Alison Stewart. U2 introduces the song "Sunday Bloody Sunday" during live concerts in Britain and Ireland.

1983

The album *War* is released and brings U2 their greatest success to date. Bono is appointed to an Irish government committee on the national unemployment problem. A concert video and recording, both called *Under a Blood Red Sky,* are released.

1984

U2 record and release *The Unforgettable Fire* album. U2 do a limited American tour with all proceeds benefiting the human rights advocacy group Amnesty International. Bono participates with other artists under the moniker Band Aid to record the song "Do They Know It's Christmas?"

1985

U2 is named "Band of the Eighties" by *Rolling Stone.* Bono and his wife Ali travel to Ethiopia to help directly in the famine relief efforts. Bono contributes to the multiartist collaboration known as Artists Against Apartheid, which opposed South African's discriminatory racial policies.

1986

Bono and Ali visit war zones in Central America.

1987

The Joshua Tree album is released and becomes a No. 1 album in both the United States and Britain.

1988

The Joshua Tree wins the Grammy award for Album of the Year. Both the film and album *Rattle and Hum* are released.

1989

Overexposure and an impression of egotism and self-seriousness cause some popular backlash against U2. Bono and the Edge write "She's a Mystery to Me" for Roy Orbison's last album. Bono's first child, daughter Jordan, is born.

1990

U2 travel to Berlin as the Berlin Wall is coming down to work on their next album. Creative differences among the members of the band cause severe tensions and threaten to break up U2.

1991

Bono's second daughter, Memphis Eve, is born. U2 finish work on their new album, *Achtung Baby.*

1992

U2 undertake the Zoo TV tour in support of their new album.

1993

U2 record another new album, *Zooropa,* in between the American and European legs of their tour and release it. Bono records and releases a duet with Frank Sinatra of the song "I've Got You Under My Skin," along with a promotional video that includes both singers.

1994

Zooropa wins the Grammy award for Best Alternative Music Album.

1995

Bono performs a duet with opera singer Luciano Pavarotti of the song "Miss Sarajevo."

1997

U2 release the album *Pop.*

1999

Bono cowrites a song and performs a duet with rap star Wyclef Jean. Bono becomes a leading proponent for Jubilee 2000, leading him to meet with world leaders of the highest caliber, including U.S. president Bill Clinton, British prime minister Tony Blair, and Pope John Paul II. Bono's third child and first son, Elijah, is born.

2000

U2 release the album *All That You Can't Leave Behind.* Bono meets with United Nations secretary general Kofi Annan on the subject of Third World debt reduction.

2001

The single "Beautiful Day" wins the Grammy award for Record of the Year and Song of the Year. U2 tour the world in support of their new album. Bono's second son and fourth child, John Abraham, is born. Bono begins a new organization called DATA to promote economic growth and relief in Africa. Bono's father, Bob Hewson, dies of cancer. U2 play a prominent role in *A Tribute to Heroes,* a television program produced to help survivors and victims' families of the September 11, 2001, terrorist attacks.

2002
U2 play the halftime show at the Super Bowl. Bono tours Africa with U.S. treasury secretary Paul O'Neill. Bono wins a human rights award from the Simon Wiesenthal Center.

2003
Bono is submitted for consideration as a candidate for the Nobel Peace Prize.

For Further Reading

Books

R.G. Grant, *Amnesty International,* World Organizations Series. New York: Franklin Watts, 2001. Provides an overview and history of the human rights organization Amnesty International, which Bono and U2 have been closely associated with for much of their careers.

Patricia McMahon, *One Belfast Boy.* Boston: Houghton Mifflin, 1999. Describes the life of a young boy trying to get away from his violence-torn hometown.

Patricia Romanowski and Holly George-Warren, eds., *The Rolling Stone Encyclopedia of Rock & Roll.* New York: Fireside, 2001. A comprehensive historical look at rock music, cataloged alphabetically by artist.

Steve Stockman, *Walk On: The Spiritual Journey of U2.* Lake Mary, Florida: Relevant Books, 2001. Examines U2's music and the members' lives, with an emphasis on their spirituality and religious beliefs.

Dave Thompson, *Bono in His Own Words.* London: Omnibus Press, 1998. A compilation of quotes by Bono on a wide range of subjects, including politics, music, and his personal life.

Websites

DATA (www.datadata.org). The official website for DATA, the organization launched by Bono to help promote trade, debt relief, and AIDS treatment and prevention in Africa.

Trouser Press (www.trouserpress.com). Now defunct, *Trouser Press* used to be a music magazine specializing in covering artists categorized as punk, new wave, or alternative/modern rock. The website contains an impressive amount of information on artists from these genres, including U2, who were considered new wave and alternative even after they became enormously popular.

VH1 (www.vh1.com). The official website for the VH1 music network. The site contains extensive pop and rock music information, including a biography and other information on U2.

Works Consulted

Books

Carter Alan, *U2: The Road to Pop*. Boston: Faber and Faber, 1997. Coverage of seventeen years of U2's history by a music industry insider who had close access and personal relationships with the band.

Mark Chatterton, *U2: The Complete Encyclopedia*. London: Firefly, 2001. Provides comprehensive information about U2, including biographies of all the band members and Bono's wife, Ali, in an accessible, alphabetized entry form.

Eamon Dunphy, *The Unforgettable Fire: Past, Present, and Future—The Definitive Biography of U2*. New York: Warner Books, 1988. A detailed biography of all the band members up until the release of *The Joshua Tree* album.

Bill Flanagan, *U2 at the End of the World*. New York: Delacorte Press, 1995. Chronicles the author's travels and the time spent with the band and those close to them during the Zoo TV and Zooropa tours and the recording of the *Zooropa* album.

Laura Jackson, *Bono: The Biography*. London: Judy Piatkus, 2001. An overview of Bono's entire life presented by a well-known British celebrity biographer.

Niall Stokes, *U2: Into the Heart: The Stories Behind Every Song*. New York: Thunder's Mouth Press, 2002. Composed by a longtime friend of U2's from Dublin, this book offers incisive information provided by the band members themselves regarding the meanings and inspirations of every song by U2.

U2: The Rolling Stone Files. New York: Rolling Stone Press, 1994. Compiled by the editors of *Rolling Stone* magazine, this book contains every article, review, and blurb on U2 from 1981 to 1993.

Periodicals

Associated Press, "Bono Offers Four-Letter Salute at Grammys," March 1, 1994.

Michael Atkinson, "Where the Streets Have No Shame," *Village Voice,* February 6, 2001.

Jay Carr, "'Million Dollar Hotel' Worth Checking Out," *Boston Globe,* May 25, 2001.

Jay Cocks, "Band on the Run," *Time,* April 27, 1987.

Alister Doyle, "Bono Named For Nobel Peace Prize," Reuters, February 18, 2003.

Amy Duncan, "U2 Sending Out Mixed Signals to Fans," *Christian Science Monitor,* November 4, 1987.

Jeff Giles, "U2 Gets Carried Away," *Newsweek,* July 12, 1993.

Tom Gliatto et al., "Bono's World," *People Weekly,* March 4, 2002.

Bill Graham, "Yep, It's U2," *Hot Press,* January 1, 1978.

Edna Gundersen, "U2's Probing 'Achtung Baby' Commands Attention," *USA Today,* December 9, 1991.

Richard Harrington, "U2 Goes over the Top with Zoo Tour," *Chicago Sun-Times,* September 14, 1992.

Richard Harrington, "When Rock Looks at War; Three New Albums Attack the Issue," *Washington Post,* April 3, 1983.

Chris Heath, "U2 Band of the Year," *Rolling Stone,* January 18, 2001.

James Hunter, *"All That You Can't Leave Behind* Review," *Rolling Stone,* November 9, 2000.

Greg Kot, "Bono's Victory," *Rolling Stone,* December 28, 2000–January 4, 2001.

Jim Miller, "Stop in the Name of Love," *Newsweek,* December 31, 1984.

New York Times, "British Soldiers Kill 13 as Rioting Erupts in Ulster," January 31, 1972.

David North, "A Delicate Balancing Act," *Maclean's,* May 13, 1985.

Sean O'Hagan, "Profile: Achtung! Saint Bono," *The Guardian* (London), November 7, 1991.

Andrew Smith, "Pop," *Sunday Times* (London), March 23, 1997.

Jim Sullivan, "Video Review: *Rattle and Hum*," *Boston Globe,* February 22, 1989.

Time, "The Bitter Road from Bloody Sunday," February 14, 1972.

Josh Tyrangiel, "Bono," *Time,* March 4, 2002.

John Waters, "Bono, Going Where No Rock Star Has Gone Before," *Irish Times,* March 4, 2002.

John Waters, "Children of Limbo," *Irish Times,* September 30, 1994.

Bernard Weinraub, "Ulster Catholics Protest Killings; Reprisals Vowed," *New York Times,* February 1, 1972.

Websites

BBC (www.bbc.co.uk). Contains extensive news and entertainment items on Bono and U2.

CNN (www.cnn.com). Includes hundreds of articles on Bono and U2.

Rock and Roll Hall of Fame (www.rockhall.com). Contains an overview of the special U2 exhibition featured at the hall beginning in February 2003.

U2 (www.U2.com). The official U2 website includes extensive information and trivia about the band, as well as the lyrics to all their songs.

White House (www.whitehouse.gov). The official White House website contains the speech President George W. Bush made after meeting with Bono at the White House.

Television Programs

Bono, Interview with John Kasich, *Heroes with John Kasich,* Fox News Channel, November 22, 2001.

Bono, Interview with Larry King, *Larry King Weekend,* CNN, December 1, 2002.

U2 concert performance on June 6, 2001, at the Fleet Center, Boston, MA, recorded for later broadcast on DIRECTV.

Radio Broadcast

A concert performance on December 17, 1981, at the Malibu nightclub in Lido Beach, New York. Recorded and broadcast by radio station WLIR-FM, Garden City, New York.

Index

Picture Credits

About the Author

David Schaffer has edited and designed books and magazines for young readers for the past eighteen years. A graduate of Skidmore College and the New York University Publishing Institute, he has written books, magazine articles, and newspaper features on history, geography, entertainment, travel, politics, and social problems confronting young people. Schaffer has been a fan of Bono and U2 for twenty years.

After spending most of his life in the New York City and Boston areas, Schaffer now lives in Upstate New York with his family.